YAS

D1607125

PIONEERS IN MATHEMATICS

MODERN MATHEMATICS

1900 to 1950

MICHAEL J. BRADLEY, PH.D.

CHELSEA HOUSE
PUBLISHERS
An imprint of Infobase Publishing

Modern Mathematics: 1900 to 1950

Copyright © 2006 by Michael J. Bradley, Ph.D.

Chelsea House
An imprint of Infobase Publishing
132 West 31st Street
New York NY 10001

Library of Congress Cataloging-in-Publication Data

Bradley, Michael J. (Michael John), 1956–
    Modern mathematics : 1900 to 1950 / Michael J. Bradley.
        p. cm.—(Pioneers in mathematics)
    Includes bibliographical references and index.
    ISBN 0-8160-5426-6 (acid-free paper)
    1. Mathematicians—Biography. 2. Mathematics—History—20th century. I.
Title.
    QA28.B736 2006
    510.92'2—dc22   2005036152

Chelsea House books are available at special discounts when purchased in bulk quantities for businesses, associations, institutions, or sales promotions. Please call our Special Sales Department in New York at (212) 967-8800 or (800) 322-8755.

You can find Chelsea House on the World Wide Web at
http://www.chelseahouse.com

Text design by Mary Susan Ryan-Flynn
Cover design by Dorothy Preston
Illustrations by Jeremy Eagle

Printed in the United States of America

MP FOF 10 9 8 7 6 5 4 3 2 1

This book is printed on acid-free paper.

CONTENTS

PREFACE

athematics is a human endeavor. Behind its numbers, equations, formulas, and theorems are the stories of the people who expanded the frontiers of humanity's mathematical knowledge. Some were child prodigies while others developed their aptitudes for mathematics later in life. They were rich and poor, male and female, well educated and self-taught. They worked as professors, clerks, farmers, engineers, astronomers, nurses, and philosophers. The diversity of their backgrounds testifies that mathematical talent is independent of nationality, ethnicity, religion, class, gender, or disability.

Pioneers in Mathematics is a five-volume set that profiles the lives of 50 individuals, each of whom played a role in the development and the advancement of mathematics. The overall profiles do not represent the 50 most notable mathematicians; rather, they are a collection of individuals whose life stories and significant contributions to mathematics will interest and inform middle school and high school students. Collectively, they represent the diverse talents of the millions of people, both anonymous and well known, who developed new techniques, discovered innovative ideas, and extended known mathematical theories while facing challenges and overcoming obstacles.

Each book in the set presents the lives and accomplishments of 10 mathematicians who lived during an historical period. *The Birth of Mathematics* profiles individuals from ancient Greece, India, Arabia, and medieval Italy who lived from 700 B.C.E. to 1300 C.E. *The Age of Genius* features mathematicians from Iran, France, England, Germany, Switzerland, and America who lived between the 14th and 18th centuries. *The Foundations of Mathematics* presents 19th-century mathematicians from various European countries. *Modern Mathematics* and *Mathematics Frontiers* profile a variety of international mathematicians who worked in the early 20th and the late 20th century, respectively.

The 50 chapters of Pioneers in Mathematics tell pieces of the story of humankind's attempt to understand the world in terms of numbers, patterns, and equations. Some of the individuals profiled contributed innovative ideas that gave birth to new branches of mathematics. Others solved problems that had puzzled mathematicians for centuries. Some wrote books that influenced the teaching of mathematics for hundreds of years. Still others were among the first of their race, gender, or nationality to achieve recognition for their mathematical accomplishments. Each one was an innovator who broke new ground and enabled their successors to progress even further.

From the introduction of the base-10 number system to the development of logarithms, calculus, and computers, most significant ideas in mathematics developed gradually, with countless individuals making important contributions. Many mathematical ideas developed independently in different civilizations separated by geography and time. Within the same civilization the name of the scholar who developed a particular innovation often became lost as his idea was incorporated into the writings of a later mathematician. For these reasons it is not always possible to identify accurately any one individual as the first person to have discovered a particular theorem or to have introduced a certain idea. But then mathematics was not created by one person or for one person; it is a human endeavor.

ACKNOWLEDGMENTS

An author does not write in isolation. I owe a debt of thanks to so many people who helped in a myriad of ways during the creation of this work.

To Jim Tanton, who introduced me to this fascinating project.

To Jodie Rhodes, my agent, who put me in touch with Facts On File and handled the contractual paperwork.

To Frank K. Darmstadt, my editor, who kept me on track throughout the course of this project.

To M. V. Moorthy, who thoroughly researched the material for the chapter on Srinivasa Iyengar Ramanujan.

To Larry Gillooly, Suzanne Scholz, and Warren Kay, who assisted with the translations of Latin, French, and German titles.

To Harry D'Souza, Alina Rudnicka-Kelly, and Kashi Bilwakesh, who provided valuable comments and additional information for several chapters.

To John Tabak, Kit Moser, Tucker McElroy, and Tobi Zausner, who shared helpful suggestions for locating sources of photographs and illustrations.

To Steve Scherwatzky, who helped me to become a better writer by critiquing early drafts of many chapters.

To Melissa Cullen-DuPont, who provided valuable assistance with the artwork.

To my wife, Arleen, who helped to find photographs and provided constant love and support.

To the many relatives, colleagues, students, and friends who inquired and really cared about my progress on this project.

To Joyce Sullivan, Donna Katzman, and their students at Sacred Heart School in Lawrence, Massachusetts, who created poster presentations for a math fair based on some of these chapters.

To the faculty and administration of Merrimack College, who created the Faculty Sabbatical Program and the Faculty Development Grant Program, both of which provided me with time to read and write.

INTRODUCTION

Modern Mathematics, the fourth volume of the Pioneers in Mathematics book set, profiles the lives of 10 mathematicians who excelled during the first half of the 20th century. They made important discoveries in both pure and applied mathematics, contributed to diverse branches of science, and participated in the development of computer technology. These individuals introduced new branches of mathematics and changed the way that mathematicians do their work.

An international community of scholars who shared their innovative ideas and worked together on joint research projects characterized mathematics in the 20th century. At the Second International Congress of Mathematicians in 1900, German mathematician David Hilbert drew his colleagues' attention to a list of 23 problems that set the research agenda for the early part of the century. Polish mathematician Wacław Sierpiński helped to establish and cultivate a productive national community of mathematicians known as the Polish school. English mathematician Godfrey Hardy brought self-taught Indian number theorist Srinivasa Iyengar Ramanujan to Cambridge University to spend five years doing research together. Hungarian mathematician Paul Erdős traveled the world writing 1,500 books and papers with 500 research collaborators. American mathematician Norbert Wiener and Hungarian mathematician John von Neumann worked with numerous scientific and engineering colleagues to produce fundamental results in physics, biology, economics, and computer technology.

For many mathematicians the realities of two world wars impacted their lives and shaped their professional careers. Sierpiński was detained as a prisoner of war during both military conflicts. World War II prevented English mathematician Grace Chisholm Young from being with her husband during the last two years of his life. At the height of her career, German Jew Amalie Emmy Noether was forced to leave her country under Adolf Hitler's Nazi regime. During World War II, English mathematician Alan Turing devised computer techniques to decipher German naval codes, while American Grace Murray Hopper developed methods to computerize the calculation of ballistics tables. Wiener created algorithms to improve the effectiveness of antiaircraft guns and von Neumann performed essential mathematical analyses for the development of atomic bombs and nuclear weapons.

The group of mathematicians profiled in this volume made influential discoveries and pioneered new branches of mathematics, science, and technology. Hilbert and Noether introduced the infinite dimensional vector spaces and algebraic rings that bear their names. Ramanujan helped lay the foundations of probabilistic number theory. Erdös contributed to the establishment of Ramsey theory and extremal theory as new branches of mathematics. Wiener was the father of cybernetics. Turing machines and von Neumann architecture laid the foundations for modern computing machines. Hopper created the first compiler program and influenced the development of the COBOL programming language for data processing.

During the first half of the 20th century, mathematics became an international discipline that led to major advances in science and technology. The 10 individuals profiled in this volume represent the thousands of scholars who made modest and momentous mathematical discoveries that contributed to this growth of knowledge. The stories of their achievements provide a glimpse into the lives and the minds of some of the pioneers who discovered mathematics.

David Hilbert

(1862–1943)

David Hilbert introduced new approaches in invariant theory, number theory, geometry, analysis, and logic and proposed a set of 23 problems that influenced the direction of mathematical research for the 20th century. (*Aufnahme von A. Schmidt, Göttingen, courtesy of AIP Emilio Segrè Visual Archives*)

Problems for a New Century

David Hilbert was a central figure in mathematics in the early 20th century, conducting research in six areas of the discipline and influencing the direction of mathematical research for the entire century. His finite basis theorem changed invariant theory from a computational discipline to an algebraic one. His report on number theory set the course for the next generation of researchers in algebraic number theory. The 21 axioms of geometry that he developed introduced a new approach to a classic area of the discipline. His introduction of infinite-dimensional Hilbert spaces played an important role in analysis and mathematical physics. The Hilbert program to establish a rigorous basis for all of mathematics was central to the development of mathematical logic. The 23 Hilbert problems that he posed at an international conference in 1900 stimulated wide-ranging mathematical research throughout the course of the 20th century.

Early Years

David Hilbert was born on January 23, 1862, in Wehlau, a small town in East Prussia near the Baltic Sea. He was the first of two children of Otto Hilbert, a county judge, and Maria Therese Erdtmann, the educated daughter of a merchant. When David's father received an appointment as a city judge a few years later, the family moved to the neighboring capital city Königsberg (present-day Kaliningrad, Russia). From 1870 to 1879 Hilbert attended school at Friedrichskolleg, a private school in Königsberg, where he studied German, Greek, Latin, history, grammar, and mathematics. He excelled in mathematics, effortlessly mastering the subject and at times explaining problems to his teachers. He completed his final year of high school at Wilhelm Gymnasium and passed the *Arbitur*, the entrance examination for German universities.

In 1880 Hilbert entered the University of Königsberg, where he concentrated exclusively on mathematics. After spending the spring semester of 1881 at the University of Heidelberg, he returned to Königsberg to complete his studies. In 1883 he met Hermann Minkowski, an 18-year-old fellow mathematics student and resident of Königsberg, who earlier that year had won the grand prize in an international mathematics competition sponsored by the French Academy of Sciences for his work on writing positive integers as sums of five perfect squares. Every afternoon at five o'clock, Hilbert, Minkowski, and Adolf Hurwitz, a new faculty member who was only three years older than Hilbert, met for a long walk and a wide-ranging discussion of mathematical ideas. The three became lifelong friends and colleagues collaborating on research projects and influencing one another's work.

Invariant Theory

Hilbert completed his coursework in 1884 and started a nine-year program of research on the topic of algebraic forms and invariant theory. He did his doctoral research under the direction of Ferdinand von Lindemann, earning his Ph.D. for a dissertation on invariant forms titled "Über invariante Eigenschaften specieller binärer Formen, insbesondere der Kugelfunctionen" (On invariant properties of special binary forms, in particular the spherical functions). After earning his doctorate he spent a semester in Leipzig studying with Felix Klein, one of Germany's most prominent mathematicians, and another semester in Paris studying with Charles Hermite and Henri Poincaré, two of France's leading mathematicians. At the end of this period of additional study, Hilbert presented a paper on invariant theory and a lecture on periodic functions to qualify for his *Habilitation*, the additional requirement needed to lecture at a German university. In the fall of 1886 he accepted a position at the University of Königsberg as a *Privatdozent* (assistant professor), allowing him to teach courses at the university, although he had to collect his fees directly from his students.

In 1888 Hilbert solved an open problem in invariant theory known as Gordan's problem by proving a property that has since been named Hilbert's basis theorem. Twenty years earlier Paul Gordan, the leading researcher in the field, had proven the existence of a finite basis for the infinite collection of binary forms—polynomials with two variables in which every term had the same degree. Hilbert proved that for any number of variables, every form could be written as a sum of a finite set of basic forms. His 1890 paper "Über die Theorie der algebraischen Formen" (On the theory of algebraic forms) published in the journal *Mathematische Annalen* (Annals of mathematics) was controversial because it proved that a finite basis existed but did not show how to construct it. Although Gordan, who reviewed the paper for the journal, criticized the proof as being theology rather than mathematics, Klein, the journal's editor, approved its publication. Two years later, after Hilbert produced a proof in which he showed how to construct a finite basis for any infinite sequence of forms, Klein described his resolution of the problem as the most important algebraic work ever published by the journal.

In the same paper in which he presented the first proof of his basis theorem, Hilbert proved another major result in invariant theory known as the *Nullstellensatz*, or zero set theorem. This theorem showed that if a polynomial p was equal to zero at the same points as all the polynomials in a set known as an ideal, then some power of p had to be a member of the ideal. This important result became a cornerstone of algebraic geometry, the branch of mathematics concerned with the study of the roots of polynomial equations.

Hilbert's papers on Gordan's problem introduced new techniques into the discipline of invariant theory, changing the emphasis from lengthy computational arguments to more streamlined algebraic proofs. His new approach resolved most of the leading questions in invariant theory and established him as one of the leading researchers in the field. He wrote a paper for the International Mathematical Congress in Chicago in 1893 in which he presented a summary of the history and current status of invariant theory. Having solved the major problem in invariant theory, he turned his attention for the next five years to a different area of mathematics —the theory of algebraic number fields.

Algebraic Number Theory

The international recognition of his research on invariant theory enabled Hilbert to advance within his profession and embrace new opportunities. His successful research earned him an appointment as associate professor at Königsberg in 1892 and a rapid promotion to full professor the following year. In October 1892 he married Käthe Jerosch, the daughter of a Königsberg merchant. He changed the focus of his research to number theory and rapidly established his reputation as a capable researcher in this area of mathematics by reproving some known results using more elegant methods. For example, in 1873 Charles Hermite had proven that the number e was transcendental, meaning that it was not the solution of a polynomial equation with integer coefficients. Using similar methods Lindemann had proven in 1882 that the number π was also transcendental. Early in 1893 Hilbert gave a simple, direct proof of the transcendental nature of both e and π. Later that year he discovered two new proofs of a more advanced idea known as the splitting of the prime ideal.

At their annual meeting in 1893, the Deutsche Mathematiker-Vereinigung (Association of German Mathematicians) asked Hilbert and Minkowski to prepare a report surveying the history and current status of research in number theory. Although Minkowski was unable to complete his portion of the project, in 1897 Hilbert presented to the society a 400-page manuscript titled *Bericht über die Theorie der algebraischen Zahlkörper* (Report on the theory of algebraic number fields). The comprehensive report he produced far exceeded the original intent of the project. In addition to collecting the results of prior research in the field, Hilbert reorganized the elements of the discipline, supplied new proofs of many results, and laid the groundwork for evolving ideas such as class field theory and relative cyclic fields. This treatise, which became known simply as the *Zahlbericht* (Number report), shaped the direction of work in number theory for the coming half-century.

During the next two years Hilbert published a sequence of papers on various topics in number theory including reciprocity laws and prime spots. In the last of these works, his 1898 paper *Über die Theorie der relativ-Abelschen Körper* (On the theory of relative abelian fields), which was published in *Jahrsbericht den Deutsche Mathematiker-Vereinigung* (Annual report of the Association of German Mathematicians), he sketched out the theory of class fields and developed the concepts and methods required for the full development of the subject, leaving a wealth of problems for other mathematicians to investigate. After publishing this paper, he turned his attention to another area of mathematics and returned to number theory only once more, 11 years later, when he proved Waring's theorem. In 1707 English mathematician Edward Waring had conjectured that every positive integer could be written as the sum of four squares, nine cubes, 19 fourth powers, and so on. In 1909 Hilbert successfully proved that for every positive integer n, there was a corresponding positive integer k for which every positive integer could be written as the sum of k integers raised to the nth power.

Geometry

In 1895 Hilbert left Königsberg to accept an appointment to the mathematics faculty at the University of Göttingen, a position that he held until his retirement 35 years later. Klein, who had moved to Göttingen 10 years earlier, was working to develop the reputation of the university's mathematics department. He attracted a faculty of capable researchers, introduced weekly seminars, and established a mathematical library. As editor in chief of the journal *Mathematische Annalen*, he solicited papers on a wide range of mathematical topics and appointed Hilbert to the editorial staff. Under the direction of Klein and Hilbert, Göttingen became the leading international center for mathematical research. After Klein's retirement in 1913, Hilbert and his former student Richard Courant established the Mathematical Institute at Göttingen, which would become the model for other research institutes in many countries.

Having reshaped invariant theory and reorganized algebraic number theory, Hilbert turned to geometry, where he accomplished a similar restructuring. In his third year at his new institution, he delivered a series of lectures on geometry that he had published in 1899 under the title *Grundlagen der Geometrie* (*Foundations of Geometry*). In this book he redeveloped all the theorems of Euclidean geometry from a fundamental set of 21 axioms that were consistent, complete, and independent. The quality of consistency meant that no combination of axioms led to a contradiction. Completeness meant that every theorem in geometry followed as a logical consequence of these 21 principles. Independence guaranteed that no one axiom was a logical consequence of the others. Hilbert insisted that all concepts in geometry must derive their properties exclusively from the axioms; no extrinsic notions could contribute to their meaning. He asserted that the validity of geometry must be retained even if one substituted the words *table*, *chair*, and *mug* for the terms *point*, *line*, and *plane*.

Hilbert's book had more influence on the subject of geometry than any other book since *Elements*, the classic work on geometry and number theory that had been written in the third century B.C.E. by Greek mathematician Euclid of Alexandria. Hilbert's treatise exerted a major influence on mathematical thought, promoting the axiomatic method for all branches of mathematics. Poincaré described the work as a classic that reestablished the stature that Euclidean geometry had lost after the discovery of non-Euclidean geometries. Hilbert's work has been translated into many languages and continues to appear in new editions, the 14th English edition having been issued in 1999.

Mathematical Problems for the Twentieth Century

At the Second International Congress of Mathematicians held in Paris in 1900, Hilbert presented a talk titled "Mathematische Problemen" (Mathematical problems) in which he identified 10 problems that he viewed as central to the progress of mathematics during the next century. The full text of his speech that circulated internationally in many mathematical journals listed 23 problems drawn from all areas of mathematics. They included six problems from the axiomatic foundations of mathematics, six from algebraic number theory, six from algebra and geometry, and five from analysis. Few of the problems were narrowly focused; most represented entire programs of research. Throughout the 20th century, the entire international mathematical community took notice each time that a mathematician solved another one of Hilbert's problems. German mathematician Hermann Weyl called the solvers the "Honors Class" of mathematics.

The first problem in the group on axiomatics, asking for a proof of the continuum hypothesis, led to fundamental results that reshaped the whole of mathematics. The continuum hypothesis, proposed by Russian-born mathematician Georg Cantor in 1879, asserted that every infinite subset of the real numbers was either countably infinite, like the set of positive integers, or had the cardinality of the continuum, like the set of all real numbers. After Ernst Zermello, Bertrand Russell, and Kurt Gödel each made significant progress on aspects of the problem, American mathematician Paul Cohen showed in 1963 that this hypothesis could not be proven from the other axioms of set theory. Although the resolution of the problem was quite different than what Hilbert had anticipated, it fully achieved the purpose he had intended by stimulating wide-ranging research in mathematics, including the questioning of basic assumptions.

Hilbert's seventh problem, one of the more specific questions on algebraic number theory, accomplished another of Hilbert's goals by generating new questions after it was solved. This problem asked for a proof that any expression of the form a^b was transcendental if a and b were algebraic numbers (the roots of polynomial equations with integer coefficients) but b was irrational (not a fraction of two integers). Numbers of this form included $2^{\sqrt{2}}$, now known as Hilbert's number. In 1934 Russian mathematician Aleksandr Gelfond produced the desired proof, and the solved problem became known as Gelfond's theorem. Broadening the scope of the original question, mathematicians asked whether a^b is transcendental if both a and b are transcendental. This more general problem remains open and continues to inspire research more than 70 years after the resolution of the original question.

The 23 Hilbert problems were more than a collection of difficult mathematical questions. In his carefully crafted speech Hilbert explained why each problem addressed an important mathematical issue. He argued that the solution to each problem would lead to theories that shed light on the particular topic and related concepts. He asserted that the existence of so many good problems was evidence of the health of the discipline of mathematics. The international mathematical community enthusiastically responded by embracing the challenge of solving his visionary problems.

Analysis and Theoretical Physics

Hilbert joined his colleagues in their work on the 23 problems he had identified. Concentrating on the last group of problems, he made analysis the focus of his research agenda from 1902 until 1912. His 1904 generalization of the Dirchlet principle helped make some progress on the 20th problem that asked for methods to find functions that take prescribed values on the boundary of a given region and whose derivatives satisfy a given partial differential equation on the interior of the region. In 1905 he provided a partial solution of the 21st problem about the existence of a linear differential equation that satisfies two specified criteria. Hilbert did wide-ranging research on the topic of calculus of variations, the branch of mathematics in which one searches for functions that satisfy a set of differential equations and that minimize the value of a related expression. His work in this area contributed to the most general of all the problems, the 23rd problem, that required extensive development of the techniques of the calculus of variations.

Hilbert's most significant contribution to analysis was his work with infinite-dimensional vector spaces, today called Hilbert spaces. These sets containing an infinite number of functions that satisfied certain convergence criteria arose in his work with integral equations, equations involving an unknown function and integrals of that function. He summarized his six years of work from 1904 to 1910 with these infinite-dimensional spaces in his book *Grundzüge einer allgemeinen Theorie der linearen Integralgleichungen* (Principles of the algebraic theory of linear integral equations), published in 1912. As his number theory report had done 15 years earlier, this treatise laid out new areas of research for generations of mathematicians.

Hilbert's work in analysis, together with his 23 problems and his accomplishments in invariant theory, number theory, and geometry, solidified his reputation as one of the leading mathematicians in the world. In 1910 the Hungarian Academy of Science awarded him their Bolyai Prize. This award, named after Hungarian geometer János Bolyai, honored Hilbert for the impact his career had made on the field of mathematics. In bestowing this tribute the academy cited the depth of his thoughts, the originality of his methods, and the rigor of his logical proofs as the outstanding characteristics of his influential body of work.

As Hilbert spaces proved to be useful in the analysis of physical phenomena, Hilbert's research next evolved into the area of mathematical physics. He made contributions to quantum mechanics, kinetic gas theory, and the theory of radiation. In 1915 he communicated daily by postcard with Albert Einstein, his colleague across campus in Göttingen's physics department, while the two worked independently to develop the field equations for the theory of general relativity. In 1924 Courant included Hilbert as coauthor of his book *Methoden der Mathematischen Physik* (*Methods of Mathematical Physics*) in which he presented the rigorous mathematical basis for a variety of theories in physics. This work and the second volume by the same title that Courant published in 1937 drew heavily from Hilbert's lectures and papers.

Foundations of Mathematics and the Infinite

In the 1920s Hilbert turned his attention to the foundations of mathematics. He started to develop a set of axioms from which all of mathematics could be logically deduced. The fundamental assumption of the "Hilbert program," as the project came to be known, was that every mathematical statement could be proved or disproved. His 1926 papers "Über das Unendliche" (On the infinite) and "Aus dem Paradies das Cantor uns geschaffen, soll uns niemand vertreiben können" (No one shall expel us from the paradise that Cantor has created for us) appearing in *Mathematicsche Annalen* showed his heavy reliance on Cantor's techniques with infinite quantities in his attempt to prove that mathematics was a discipline free from contradiction. He further explained this connection in the 1928 book *Grundzüge der theoretischen Logik* (*Principles of Mathematical Logic*) that he wrote with Wilhelm Ackermann. Gödel's 1931 proof of the incompleteness theorem—the principle that every axiomatic mathematical system included propositions that could neither be proved or disproved—rendered the goals of the Hilbert program impossible.

Throughout his career Hilbert maintained a strong interest in Cantor's ideas of infinity. As early as 1891, in a paper titled "Über die stetige Abbildung einer Linie auf ein Flachenstück" (On the continuous mapping of a line into a planar region) that appeared in *Mathematische Annalen*, he demonstrated that a one-dimensional curve could have as many points as a two-dimensional region. He presented an iterative method for creating a space-filling curve that passed through every point inside a square. Starting with a curve formed by three line segments in the shape of an upside down U, he replaced the entire curve by four smaller U-shapes connected by

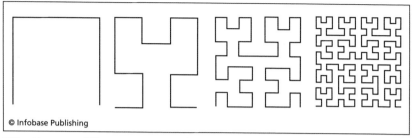

Hilbert's space-filling curve passes through every point inside a square. To construct the curve, start with a U-shaped curve formed by three line segments and replace the entire curve by four smaller U shapes connected by three shorter line segments. In each subsequent step make similar replacements resulting in four times as many of the fundamental U shapes. The Hilbert curve is the limit of an infinite sequence of steps.

three shorter line segments. In each subsequent step he made similar replacements resulting in four times as many of the fundamental U shapes. He demonstrated that the limiting curve in this infinite sequence of images called a fractal would pass through every point in the square.

In discussions with other mathematicians about the idea of infinity, Hilbert posed several paradoxes about a hotel with infinitely many rooms numbered 1, 2, 3, ... He explained that even if all the rooms were occupied the hotel's manager could accommodate one more guest by moving each existing guest into the next higher-numbered room. His solution to move the occupant of room n to room $n + 1$ for every positive integer n guaranteed every person a new room and made the first room available for the new guest. If k people arrived, the manager could move the guest in room n to room $n + k$. Stretching the problem further, Hilbert suggested that if a train arrived with infinitely many new guests, the manager could accommodate them by moving the current occupant of room n to room $2n$, making all the odd-numbered rooms available for the new guests. He even suggested that if an infinite number of trains arrived, the manager could move the existing resident of room n to room 2^n leaving rooms 3, 3^2, 3^3, . . . for the new guests in the first train, rooms 5, 5^2, 5^3, . . . for the new guests in the second train, rooms 7, 7^2, 7^3, . . . for the new guests in the third train, and so on, with a new prime number for each additional train. "Hilbert's hotel," as the paradoxical setting came to be called, provided tangible examples of the arithmetic of infinite quantities that Cantor had introduced into set theory.

Wars and Retirement

In 1930, when Hilbert reached the mandatory retirement age of 68, he delivered his farewell lecture on invariant theory to a packed auditorium of professors and students, a marked contrast to the winter semester of 1891–92 at Königsberg when only a single student had signed up for his course on complex function theory. During his career he had supervised the doctoral dissertations of 69 students. Weyl, his former student and his successor as head of the Mathematical Institute at Göttingen, likened him to the Pied Piper, having lured so many innocent young minds into the deep river of mathematics. He was popular with both the faculty and the students and shunned the formality of tradition to freely socialize with and work with both groups. At conferences and lectures he sat with the young faculty members. At parties he danced with their wives. On occasion he arrived in his lecture hall on his skis or his bicycle. He invited visitors at his home to grab a piece of chalk and attempt to solve a problem on the 18-foot blackboard that he had mounted on the wall in his backyard.

An outspoken individual with strongly held beliefs, Hilbert had made his opinions known throughout his career. In 1914 he had defied government authorities by refusing to sign the Declaration to the Cultural World, a document that sought to absolve Germany and the kaiser of all responsibility for the atrocities of World War I. In 1917, while German and French soldiers were fighting each other during the war, he published an obituary in *Mathematische Annalen* honoring deceased French mathematician Gaston Darboux. He supported female mathematician Emmy Noether's appointment to the faculty at Göttingen, declaring at a faculty meeting that her gender was not a relevant issue since this was a university, not a bathhouse. Adolf Hitler's decision to remove all Jewish faculty members from German universities in the early 1930s decimated the Mathematical Institute at Göttingen, which until then had been the leading international center for mathematical research. In 1935, when the Nazi minister of education asked Hilbert about the state of mathematics at Göttingen, he replied that there was no more mathematics at Göttingen.

During the 1930s Hilbert and his colleagues published several volumes of his mathematical research. In 1932 with Stefan Cohn-Vossen he wrote *Anschauliche Geometrie* (*Geometry and the Imagination*), a descriptive survey of the geometry of curves and surfaces. In 1934 and 1939 with Paul Bernays he published a two-volume treatise titled *Grundlagen der Mathematik* (*Foundations of Mathematics*) on the axiomatization of mathematics. As Courant had done with the two-volume treatise on mathematical physics, Cohn-Vossen and Bernays based these two works on lectures Hilbert had given in the early 1920s and included his name as coauthor although they did almost all of the writing. All three coauthored works were translated into multiple languages and distributed internationally. Between 1932 and 1935 Hilbert collected his papers on number theory, algebra, and analysis and published them as the three-volume work *Gesammelte Abhandlungen* (Collected works).

In the last year of his life, Hilbert's physical activity was limited by a broken arm that he had sustained during a fall on a Göttingen street. He died on February 14, 1943. Due to the war, less than a dozen people attended his funeral service at his home.

Conclusion

David Hilbert influenced multiple areas of mathematics through his research and through his visionary set of 23 problems. The methods he used to solve Gordan's problem and establish his finite basis theorem transformed invariant theory from a computational discipline to an algebraic one. His *Zahlbericht* set the course for the next generation of researchers in algebraic number theory. His book on the foundations of geometry dominated the approach to that area of mathematics for the next half-century. In analysis and mathematical physics, his introduction of infinite-dimensional Hilbert spaces played an important role. Although the Hilbert program to axiomatize all of mathematics did not reach its ultimate goal, his work on mathematical logic contributed to the rigorous development of many branches of the discipline. The 23 Hilbert problems that he challenged his colleagues to solve successfully stimulated wide-ranging mathematical research throughout the course of the 20th century, as he had intended.

FURTHER READING

Drucker, Thomas. "David Hilbert, 1862–1943, German Number Theorist." In *Notable Mathematicians: From Ancient Times to the Present*, edited by Robyn V. Young, 244–247. Detroit, Mich.: Gale, 1998. Brief but informative profile of Hilbert and his work.

Freudenthal, Hans. "Hilbert, David." In *Dictionary of Scientific Biography*, Vol. 6, edited by Charles C. Gillispie, 388–395. New York: Scribner, 1972. Encyclopedic biography, including a detailed description of his mathematical writings.

Gray, Jeremy J. *The Hilbert Challenge*. Oxford: Oxford University Press, 2000. Biography of Hilbert's early career leading to the 23 Hilbert problems; for a more advanced audience.

Joyce, D. "The Mathematical Problems of David Hilbert." Clark University. Available online. URL: http://babbage.clarku.edu/~djoyce/hilbert. Accessed August 2, 2005. Article about Hilbert, with links to the full text of his 1900 speech on his 23 problems and to two additional articles giving the progress on each problem after 100 years.

O'Connor, J. J., and E. F. Robertson. "David Hilbert." MacTutor History of Mathematics Archive, University of Saint Andrews. Available online. URL: http://www-groups.dcs.st-andrews.ac.uk/~history/Mathematicians/Hilbert.html. Accessed August 2, 2005. Biography provided by the University of Saint Andrews, Scotland.

Reid, Constance. *Hilbert*. New York: Springer-Verlag, 1970. Biography of Hilbert with a balance of personal information and mathematics.

Grace Chisholm Young

2

(1868–1944)

Grace Chisholm Young wrote papers on infinite derivatives and nondifferentiable functions. She also coauthored books on set theory and the geometry of paper folding. *(Sydney Jones Library, the University of Liverpool)*

Mathematical Partnership

Grace Chisholm Young was the first woman to earn a doctoral degree from a German university through the standard process of coursework, examination, and dissertation. Her papers on infinite derivatives and nondifferentiable functions won the Gamble Prize and established a portion of the Denjoy-Saks-Young theorem. With her mathematician husband she coauthored a children's book on the geometry of paper folding, an influential book on set theory, and more than 200 papers on various topics in mathematics.

Early Life and Education

Grace Emily Chisholm was born on March 15, 1868, in Haslemere, England, a town in Sussex County, southwest of London. Henry William Chisholm, her father, served as warden of the standards supervising the government's department of weights and measures. Anna Louisa Bell, her mother, was an accomplished pianist who performed in public recitals. Unlike their older brother, Hugh, who attended grammar school, a private boarding school, and Oxford University, Grace and her older sister, Helen, received their early education at home from their mother. The young Grace suffered from headaches and nightmares, and her doctors recommended that her parents teach Grace only those subjects in which she expressed an interest. Accordingly, her education focused primarily on music and mathematics until she was 10 years old, when her health improved and her parents hired a governess to teach her a fuller range of subjects. At the age of 17 she passed the entrance exam for Cambridge University. She hoped to study medicine at the university, but in accordance with her parents' wishes, she instead became involved in social work among the poor in London.

Chisholm eventually persuaded her parents to allow her to study mathematics, and she applied to Cambridge University's Girton College, an institution established in 1869 as England's first residential college for women. At the age of 21 she entered Girton as the institution's Sir Francis Goldsmid Scholar of Mathematics. In 1892, after completing her coursework, she passed the Mathematical Tripos, comprehensive examinations that determined the students' final class rankings at graduation. Chisholm placed 23rd among the top-scoring group of students who graduated with the equivalent of a bachelor's degree. In addition, Chisholm unofficially took the final mathematics examination at Oxford University, finishing with the highest score for all students at Oxford that year. Yet, despite her performance she did not receive a formal degree; women were permitted to take courses at Cambridge but were not granted official degrees.

In the course of Chisholm's studies at Girton, she met William Henry Young, one of the college's mathematics tutors and her future husband. Young, who was five years older than Chisholm, had earned his degree in mathematics from Cambridge University in 1884. He was a fellow at Cambridge's Peterhouse College from 1886 to 1892 and tutored students in preparation for the Tripos. He served as Chisholm's tutor for one of her years at Girton, directing her studies and preparing her for her examinations.

After completing her coursework at Girton, Chisholm wanted to continue her education in mathematics, but universities in England did not permit women to take graduate-level courses. In 1893 she obtained permission from the Berlin Ministry of Culture to enroll at the University of Göttingen, in Germany, where the faculty had recently established a course for women in mathematics, physics, and astronomy. Under the direction of Felix Klein, she completed a doctoral dissertation titled "Algebraisch-gruppentheoretische Untersuchungen zur sphärischen Trigonometrie" (Algebraic group theoretic examination on spherical trigonometry). Her research focused on properties associated with the sines and cosines of the angles in a triangle drawn on the surface of a sphere. In August 1895 she received her Ph.D. with the distinction magna cum laude (with high honors), becoming the first woman to earn a doctoral degree from a German university by completing the standard program of formal coursework, doctoral examination, and written thesis.

Partners in Life and in Mathematics

After receiving her degree, Chisholm returned to England to care for her 86-year-old father and 71-year-old mother. She sent a copy of her doctoral thesis to Young, her former tutor. Impressed by her work he invited her to coauthor an astronomy book with him. The two mathematicians developed a close relationship and married in June 1896. During their first year of marriage they lived at Cambridge University, where she conducted mathematical research, while he taught classes. Although they never completed the proposed astronomy book, her paper "On the Curve $y = (x^2 + \sin^2 \psi)^{-3/2}$, and Its Connection with an Astronomical Problem" appeared in 1897 in the *Monthly Notices, Royal Astronomical Society* under the name "Mrs. W. H. Young [Miss Grace Chisholm]."

When her thesis adviser Klein visited Cambridge in 1897 to accept an honorary degree, he encouraged Young and her husband to devote their talents to joint mathematical research. After the birth of their first child, Francis, later that year, they moved to Göttingen and became active members of the mathematical research community, as Klein had suggested. The next 32 years they collaborated on more than 200 articles and several books covering a range of topics in mathematics, academia, and education. Although most of their early work was published only in her husband's name, Grace Young was an equal partner in their research collaboration, developing creative ideas, constructing detailed proofs, and corresponding with publishers.

After spending a year in Turin, Italy, Young and her husband returned to Göttingen, where they stayed until 1908. During those years they had five more children: three daughters named Cecily, Janet, and Helen and two sons named Laurence and Patrick. Young, who taught her children at home, wrote three books on mathematics and science for young people. In 1905 she and her husband wrote *The First Book of Geometry* in which they used paper-folding projects to introduce children to elementary concepts of geometry involving angles, symmetry, surface areas, and volumes of three-dimensional figures. The book was translated into German, Italian, and Hebrew during the next 16 years and was rereleased in the United States in 1969. Young independently wrote two science books whose titles incorporated her oldest son's nickname. *Bimbo*, published in 1905, and *Bimbo and the Frogs*, published two years later, introduced children to biology by providing simple scientific explanations of the facts of reproduction, including the process of cell division.

In addition to writing books for children, Young and her husband coauthored an advanced mathematics text titled *The Theory of Sets of Points*. Published in 1906, their book presented the first systematic exposition of set theory, a new branch of mathematics recently introduced by Russian mathematician Georg Cantor. Their detailed treatise introduced formal definitions of technical terms associated with sets of points in one and two dimensions. For an interval $[a, b]$ on the real line, they defined a point to be an internal point if it was not one of the endpoints of the interval. They designated a point x to be a limit point of a set of points if every interval containing x as an internal point included other points of the set. Building on these definitions, they defined a set to be closed if it contained all its limit points and unclosed if it did not. For regions in the plane, they distinguished internal points, boundary points, and external points based on whether triangles containing the points were completely inside the region, included some points in the region, or were completely outside the region, respectively. They redefined Cantor's definition of a connected set in terms of limit points rather than using his idea of the minimal distance between points in the set. With these new definitions they reformulated and proved known theorems about sets of points in the real line and generalized them to corresponding statements about regions in the plane.

The ideas the Youngs presented in *The Theory of Sets of Points* impacted other branches of mathematics. The couple demonstrated that the techniques in the developing area of set theory could be applied to many established branches of mathematics, including projective geometry, complex function theory, calculus of variations, and differential equations. Their careful definitions and reworking of informal concepts provided a more rigorous foundation for a

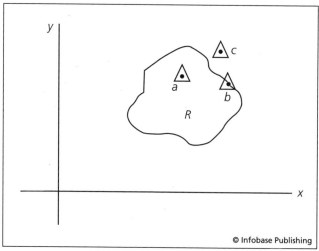

© Infobase Publishing

In their book *The Theory of Sets of Points*, the Youngs introduced formal definitions for many fundamental concepts in set theory. For a region R in the x-y plane, a point a was an internal point if some triangle containing a was composed only of points in R. A point b was a boundary point if every triangle containing b included points in R and points not in R. A point c was an external point if some triangle containing c included no points of R.

number of concepts that became important in topology, the branch of mathematics dealing with the properties of geometrical surfaces. Cantor commented enthusiastically on their joint work, praising the Youngs for their diligence, skill, and acuteness of mind.

The theory of sets continued to play a central role in the Youngs' research for many years. Their 1914 paper "On the Reduction of Sets of Intervals," published in the *Proceedings of the London Mathematical Society*, presented results about intervals on the one-dimensional real line. They discussed sets of points in two-dimensional space in their 1916 paper "Sur la frontière normale d'une région ou d'un ensemble" (On the normal frontier of a region or of a set), which appeared in the French journal *Comptes rendus hebdomadaires des séances de l'Académie des Sciences* (Rendering of the accounts of the weekly sessions of the Academy of Sciences). Their 1917 paper "On the Internal Structure of a Set of Points in Space of Any Number of Dimensions," published in the *Proceedings of the London Mathematical Society*, analyzed sets in higher dimensional spaces. Other papers that the Youngs wrote collaboratively and independently contributed important results to the theory of cluster sets and prime sets.

Young and her husband engaged in a fruitful mathematical partnership despite frequent periods of separation. William held a sequence of positions as an examiner at Cambridge University, the University of London, and the University of Wales and later became a part-time mathematics professor at Calcutta University, the University of Liverpool, and University College in Wales. When they were apart, Young and her husband wrote frequent letters to each other accompanied by drafts of mathematical manuscripts. When they were together, they worked so hard on their research that Grace often became exhausted and slept for several days after William had left. When her husband was out of town, one of her two unmarried sisters-in-law often came to live with Young, enabling her to work on her own research and writing and, at times, to accompany her husband on some of his trips abroad.

In addition to conducting mathematical research, Young maintained a variety of other interests. Pursuing her dream to become a physician, she studied medicine at the University of Göttingen. When she and her husband moved their family to Geneva,

Switzerland, in 1908, she continued her studies at the University of Geneva, where she completed all the requirements for a degree in medicine with the exception of an internship. She also learned to speak six languages and taught each of her children how to play a musical instrument.

Independent Work on Infinite Derivatives

Between 1914 and 1916 Young produced her most significant independent mathematical work. During this period she wrote several papers on the foundations of differential calculus that were published under her own name in an assortment of international journals. Her 1914 paper "A Note on Derivatives and Differential Coefficients," which appeared in the Swedish journal *Acta Mathematica* (Mathematical activities), presented some of her preliminary results on particular properties of derivatives. In 1915 her essay "On Infinite Derivatives" won the Gamble Prize from Girton College. Published in 1916 in the *Quarterly Journal of Pure and Applied Mathematics*, this lengthy treatise discussed functions that were continuous but were not differentiable. She continued this research theme with the short paper "Sur les nombres dérivés d'une function" (On the numbers derived from a function), which appeared in the same year in the journal *Comptes rendus hebdomadaires des séances de l'Académie des Sciences*.

In 1916 the *Proceedings of the London Mathematical Society* published Young's paper titled "On the Derivatives of a Function" in which she discussed four variations of the classical derivative of a function known as the upper left, lower left, upper right, and lower right Dini derivatives. In this paper she categorized the behavior of the four Dini derivatives for continuous functions and for measurable functions. She showed that except at a small set of points, the four Dini derivatives had to behave in one of three ways: they were all equal; two were positively infinite, and two were negatively infinite; or one was positively infinite, another was negatively infinite, and the other two were equal to some common finite value. The results she proved, together with similar results obtained by the French mathematician Arnaud Denjoy and the Polish mathematician Stanisław Saks, became known as the Denjoy-Saks-Young theorem. The theorem allows researchers to use a process of elimination to show that a particular function is differentiable by demonstrating that the second and third cases do not occur.

The Young family's move from Geneva to Lausanne, also in Switzerland, in 1915 did not slow Grace's research productivity. She continued to generate publishable research results on calculus through the end of the 1920s. She wrote about Lebesgue integrals in a 1919 paper titled "Démonstration du lemme de Lebesgue sans l'emploi des nombres de Cantor" (Demonstration of Lebesgue's lemma without the use of the Cantor numbers), which appeared in the *Bulletin des sciences mathématiques* (Bulletin of the mathematical sciences). Her 1922 paper on Riemann integrals, titled "A Note on a Theorem of Riemann's," was published in the *Messenger of Mathematics.* In 1922 she wrote about multivariable calculus in the paper "On the Partial Derivatives of a Function of Many Variables," which was published in the *Proceedings of the London Mathematical Society.* The journal *Fundamenta Mathematicae* (Fundamentals of mathematics) published her 1929 paper "On Functions Possessing Differentials."

Young's writings in the 1920s addressed additional mathematical topics beyond calculus. Two of her papers were inspired by mathematical ideas contained in the writings of the ancient Greek philosopher Plato. In 1924 she wrote "On the Solution of a Pair of Simultaneous Diophantine Equations Connected with the Nuptial Number in Plato," published in the *Proceedings of the London Mathematical Society.* Five years later she cowrote with her husband "A Time-Honoured Mystery from the Meno of Plato," which appeared in the journal *O Instituto* (O tradition). In 1926 she wrote an expository article for an educational journal explaining the Greek mathematician Pythagoras's proof of his famous theorem that related the lengths of the sides of a right triangle. The paper "Pythagore, comment a-t-il trouvé son théorème?" (Pythagoras. How did he prove his theorem?) appeared in *L'Enseignement mathématique* (Mathematics education).

Final Years of Her Career

While Young was earning an international reputation as a research mathematician, her husband was also receiving honors for his work.

In 1907 William was elected a fellow of the Royal Society, Britain's academy of science. His influential 1910 textbook, *The Fundamental Theorems of the Differential Calculus,* introduced a new approach to functions of several variables that all advanced calculus books have since employed. In recognition of his contributions to mathematics, he received the 1917 DeMorgan Medal from the London Mathematical Society and the 1928 Sylvester Medal from the Royal Society. He served as president of the London Mathematical Society from 1922 to 1924 and as president of the International Mathematical Union from 1929 to 1936.

By the end of the 1920s both Young and her husband had ceased their mathematical research. In 1929 Grace started a five-year project to write a 16th-century historical novel titled *The Crown of England* but never completed the work. In 1940, at the beginning of World War II, she flew to England with two of her grandchildren, intending to return to Switzerland. Unable to rejoin her husband because of the war, she stayed in England, while he remained in Switzerland. Isolated and separated from his family, William became depressed and died in 1942. Young lived in England for another two years until she died of a heart attack at her daughter's house in Croydon, in 1944. The fellows at Girton College had decided to award her an honorary degree, but she died before the ceremony could be arranged.

All six of the Youngs' children earned college degrees, three of them in mathematics. Laurence and Cecily became mathematics professors. Janet earned a medical degree and became the first female member of the Royal College of Surgeons. The Youngs' granddaughter Sylvia Wiegand continues the family legacy today as a professor of mathematics at the University of Nebraska.

Conclusion

During a 40-year career in which she never held a formal appointment, Grace Chisholm Young established a solid reputation as a research mathematician. She was the first woman to earn a doctoral degree from a German university through the standard process of coursework, examination, and dissertation. Her paper on continuous, nondifferentiable functions won the Gamble Prize from

Girton College. Her discoveries about infinite Dini derivatives proved a portion of the Denjoy-Saks-Young theorem in calculus. With her husband she cowrote a children's book on the geometry of paper folding and an influential book on set theory. During their prolific collaboration they produced more than 200 papers in various branches of mathematics.

FURTHER READING

Koch, Laura Coffin. "Grace Chisholm Young." In *Notable Women in Mathematics: A Biographical Dictionary*, edited by Charlene Morrow and Teri Perl, 277–282. Westport, Conn.: Greenwood Press, 1998. Short biography of Young.

O'Connor, J. J., and E. F. Robertson. "Grace Chisholm Young." MacTutor History of Mathematics Archive, University of Saint Andrews. Available online. URL: http://www-groups.dcs.st-andrews.ac.uk/~history/Mathematicians/Chisholm_Young.html. Accessed August 12, 2005. Biography provided by the University of Saint Andrews, Scotland.

Perl, Teri. "Grace Chisholm Young." In *Math Equals: Biographies of Women Mathematicians + Related Activities*, 148–171. Menlo Park, Calif.: Addison-Wesley, 1978. Biography accompanied by exercises related to her mathematical work.

Pyenson, Lewis. "Grace Chisholm Young, 1868–1944, English Applied Mathematician." In *Notable Mathematicians: From Ancient Times to the Present*, edited by Robyn V. Young, 521–522. Detroit, Mich.: Gale, 1998. Brief but informative profile of Young and her work.

Riddle, Larry. "Grace Chisholm Young." Agnes Scott College. Available online. URL: http://www.agnesscott.edu/lriddle/women/young.htm. Accessed August 13, 2005. Online article detailing Young's life and work.

Weigand, Sylvia M. "Grace Chisholm Young (1868–1944)." In *Women of Mathematics: A Biobibliographic Sourcebook*, edited by Louise S. Grinstein and Paul J. Campbell, 247–254. New York: Greenwood Press, 1987. Biographical profile with an evaluation of her mathematics, written by her granddaughter and including an extensive list of references.

3

Wacław Sierpiński

(1882–1969)

Wacław Sierpiński developed fractal patterns in set theory, introduced new categories of integers in number theory, discovered the first absolutely normal number, and helped to establish the Polish school of mathematics. (Archives of the Polish Academy of Sciences)

Number Theory and the Polish School of Mathematics

In a career that spanned 60 years, Wacław Sierpiński (pronounced shur-PIN-skee) wrote 50 books and more than 700 research papers. In the fields of set theory and topology, he discovered many relationships between the continuum hypothesis and properties of metric spaces. His Sierpiński snowflake and Sierpiński triangle provided early examples of fractal patterns. In number theory he introduced Sierpiński numbers of the first and second kind, investigated properties of prime numbers, and discovered the first absolutely normal number. Despite incarceration twice as a prisoner of war, he was a leader in the Polish school of mathematics, helping to establish research institutions, specialized journals, and professional societies.

Early Work in Number Theory

Wacław Franciszek Sierpiński was born on March 14, 1882, in Warsaw, Poland, to Constantine Sierpiński, a prominent physician, and Louise Lapinska. As a high school student he demonstrated strong mathematical abilities and helped organize free courses for boys who could not afford to attend formal schools. In 1900 he enrolled as a student of mathematics and physics at the Czar's University, formerly known as the University of Warsaw, where the Russian government that ruled Poland at the time had replaced all faculty members with Russian professors and had mandated that all classes were to be taught in the Russian language. The university's academic and political environment nourished his talent for mathematics and his commitment to Polish nationalism.

Sierpiński studied under the guidance of Georgy Voronoy, an accomplished Russian mathematician who influenced his early research. In 1903 he won a gold medal in the department's competition for the best student essay on Voronoy's contributions to number theory, the mathematical study of the properties of positive integers. His paper "O pewnym zagadnieniu z rachunku funkcji asymptotycznych" (On a problem of the theory of asymptotic functions) was scheduled to be printed in the university's journal, but Sierpiński, who did not want his first work to be printed in Russian, had it withdrawn. The paper instead appeared in 1906 in the Polish journal *Prace Matematyczne-Fizyczne* (The works of mathematics and physics).

Sierpiński's prize-winning paper concerned the quantity $R(r)$ that represented the number of points with integer coordinates that lie inside or on the boundary of a circle of radius r. In 1837 German mathematician Carl Friedrich Gauss had shown that $R(r)$ provided an estimate for the area of the circle that differed from the actual value of πr^2 by a constant multiple of the

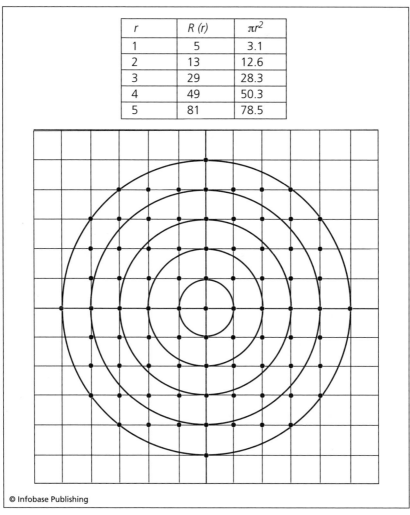

r	$R(r)$	πr^2
1	5	3.1
2	13	12.6
3	29	28.3
4	49	50.3
5	81	78.5

© Infobase Publishing

In a prize-winning paper Sierpiński investigated the quantity $R(r)$, the number of points with integer coordinates that lie on or inside the circle of radius r. This chart shows that for circles of radii r = 1, 2, 3, 4, and 5, this quantity closely approximates the area of the circle that is given by the formula $A = \pi r^2$.

radius. This theorem led to a more general question known as the Gauss circle problem, which asked for the minimum value of k for which $\left| R(r) - \pi r^2 \right| < Cr^k$. Sierpiński's proof that $k \leq 2/3$ was a significant improvement on Gauss's result of $k = 1$. Although mathematicians have continued to analyze this question, the most recent bound of $k \le 46/73$ that Welsh mathematician Martin N. Huxley obtained in 1990 represents only a slight improvement over Sierpiński's work.

During his final year at the university, Sierpiński made a political statement by refusing to answer any questions on the Russian-language examination that was required for graduation. The sympathetic examiner gave him a passing grade, allowing him to graduate in 1904 with the degree "candidate of sciences," the equivalent of a bachelor of science degree. He taught mathematics and physics at a girls' school in Warsaw until the Russian revolution of 1905, when he participated in a school strike, resigned his teaching position, and entered the graduate program in mathematics at the Jagiellonian University in Kraków, Poland. In 1908 he earned his Ph.D. for a doctoral dissertation titled "O sumowaniu szeregu $\sum \tau(n) f(n)$, gdzie $\tau(n)$ oznacza liczbę rozktadow liczbę n na sumę kwadratów dwóch liczb calkowitych" (On the summation of the series $\sum \tau(n) f(n)$, where $\tau(n)$ denotes the number of decompositions of n into a sum of two squares of integers). In this work, which was published later that year in *Prace Matematyczne-Fizyczne*, he determined the values of several infinite summations involving the number of ways to write a positive integer as the sum of two squares.

Between 1904 and 1910 Sierpiński published 18 papers on number theory. Half of these research papers were in the area of analytic number theory involving the representation of integers as sums or differences of two squares. An equal number of papers from the area of Diophantine analysis addressed the problem of finding integer solutions to polynomial equations. In his 1909 paper titled "O pewnym twierdzeniu z teorii przybliżeń wymiernych" (On a theorem in the theory of Diophantine approximation), which appeared in *Comptes rendus de la Société des Sciences de Varsovie* (Rendering of the accounts of the Society of Sciences of Warsaw), Sierpiński investigated the number of fractions whose values closely approximated a given decimal quantity. He proved that if x is a real number and n is a positive integer, then there are at most two fractions $\frac{p}{q}$ with $1 \le q \le n$ for which $\left| x - \frac{p}{q} \right| < \frac{1}{nq}$. For the values $x = 3.71$ and $n = 5$, his result meant that the fractions $\frac{15}{4} = 3.75$ and $\frac{11}{3} \approx 3.67$

were the only two fractions that satisfied the required inequality. Problems like these, whose solutions illustrated fundamental properties of mathematics, attracted his attention throughout his career.

In addition to his research papers, Sierpiński published two books on number theory during this early phase of his career. *Teoria liczb niewymiernych* (The theory of irrational numbers), published in 1910, and *Teoria liczb* (The theory of numbers), published in 1911, were part of a series of books collectively titled *Poradnik dla Samouków* (Guidebooks for self-instruction). This initiative was one of several projects funded by the Mianowski Foundation that enabled Polish scholars to circumvent governmental restrictions and provide Polish students with high-quality textbooks on current topics.

Research on Set Theory

From 1908 to 1914 Sierpiński taught as a member of the mathematics faculty at Jan Kazimierz University in Lwów, Poland (present-day Lviv, Ukraine), where he became an assistant professor in 1908 and an associate professor in 1910. In Lwów his research interests turned to set theory, a new branch of mathematics that Russian mathematician Georg Cantor had introduced in the 1870s. Drawing on disparate ideas that Cantor and other set theorists had presented in their papers and books, Sierpiński developed an organized approach to the general theory of sets. In 1909 he delivered one of the first systematic lecture courses in set theory given at any university. His 1912 book *Zarys teorii mngości* (Outline of set theory), based on his lecture notes for this course, became a popular textbook throughout Europe and earned an award from the Polish Academy of Sciences in Kraków.

The problem that stimulated Sierpiński's original interest in set theory was Cantor's 1878 paper establishing a one-to-one correspondence between the points in the unit square $S = \{(x, y) \mid 0 \le x, y \le 1\}$ and the points in the unit interval $I = \{z \mid 0 \le z \le 1\}$. Sierpiński introduced an alternative variation on this idea in his 1912 paper "Sur une nouvelle courbe continué qui remplit toute une aire plane" (On a new continuous curve that completely fills a plane area), which appeared in the *Bulletin de l'Académie des Sciences Cracovie* (Bulletin of the Academy of Sciences of Kraków). The Sierpiński curve, or Sierpiński snowflake, that he developed was a closed path that passed through every point in the interior of the unit square. This space-filling curve that mapped a one-dimensional interval into a two-dimensional area had infinite length and enclosed an area of $\frac{5}{12}$. The Sierpiński curve is an example of a fractal, a recursively defined geometrical object in which each section of the pattern is similar to the entire design.

When World War I started, in 1914, Russian military authorities detained Sierpiński as a prisoner of war in Vyatka, Russia. Through the intercession of Russian mathematicians Nikolai Luzin and Dimitri Egorov, he was relocated to a facility near Moscow University. This arrangement allowed him to continue his own work and to conduct joint research with his Russian colleagues in set-theoretic topology and the theory of analytic and projective sets.

His 1915 paper "Sur une courbe dont tout point est un point de ramification" (On a curve for which every point is a ramification point) appearing in the French journal *Comptes rendus mathématiques de l'Académie des Sciences* (Rendering of the mathematical accounts of the Academy of Sciences) introduced another fractal known as the Sierpiński triangle, the Sierpiński sieve, or the Sierpiński gasket. The image is derived from an equilateral triangle

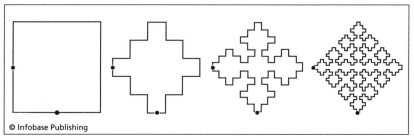

© Infobase Publishing

The Sierpiński curve, also known as the Sierpiński snowflake, is a one-dimensional curve that passes through every point inside a square. To construct the curve, each L-shaped corner piece of a square must be replaced by a linked sequence of five shorter corner pieces. In each subsequent step, similar replacements result in five times as many of the fundamental L shapes. The Sierpiński curve is the limit of an infinite sequence of steps.

by cutting it into four equal triangles, removing the central piece, and repeatedly applying the same procedure to each remaining triangle. Sierpiński showed that after n iterations there are 3^n triangles and that the side of each triangle is $\left(\dfrac{1}{2}\right)^n$ as long as a side of the original triangle. The total area and perimeter of the collection of triangles are $\left(\dfrac{3}{4}\right)^n$ and $3\left(\dfrac{3}{2}\right)^n$ of the corresponding dimensions of the original triangle.

Ever since he published this paper, Sierpiński's triangle has inspired geometers who study fractal images to design several related objects that they have named in his honor. The two-dimensional Sierpiński carpet is constructed from a square by cutting it into nine equal squares, removing the central piece, and repeatedly applying the same procedure to each remaining square. Its three-dimensional analog, known as the Sierpiński sponge, is constructed by subdividing a cube into 27 equal cubes, removing the central piece, and replicating the process with each smaller cube. Repeatedly subdividing a pyramid with a triangular base into five similar shapes and removing the central piece produces the Sierpiński tetrahedron, the three-dimensional generalization of the Sierpiński triangle. The graphical and numerical capabilities of computers have further stimulated interest in the early 20th-century work of Sierpiński and his contemporaries.

Sierpiński's work with sets of numbers led him to the discovery of the first absolutely normal number, a real number whose digits

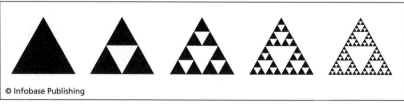

© Infobase Publishing

The Sierpiński triangle is constructed from an equilateral triangle by cutting it into four equal triangles, removing the central piece, and repeatedly applying the same procedure to each remaining triangle.

occur with equal frequency in every number base. In 1909 French mathematician Émile Borel had proven the existence of such numbers. Sierpiński gave the first example of an absolutely normal number in his 1917 paper "Démonstration élémentaire d'un théorème de M. Borel sur les nombres absolument normaux et détermination effective d'un tel nombre" (Elementary demonstration of a theorem of Mr. Borel on absolutely normal numbers and the effective determination of one such number), which appeared in the *Bulletin de la Société Mathématique de France* (Bulletin of the Mathematical Society of France). Sierpiński developed an intricate construction of his number as the lower bound of a well-defined set of real numbers. Mathematicians have not yet discovered a general method to determine whether a given number is absolutely normal.

Polish School of Mathematics

When Sierpiński regained his freedom in 1918, at the end of World War I, he assumed a leadership role within the Polish mathematical community. After a brief return to Jan Kazimierz University, he accepted an appointment at the University of Warsaw, where he was promoted to full professor in 1919 and dean of the faculty in 1921. With Zygmunt Janiszewski and Stefan Mazurkiewicz, he formulated and implemented a plan to create an active community of research mathematicians in Poland that became known as the Polish school of mathematics. The three established the University of Warsaw as the country's mathematical research center, assembling a strong faculty and attracting a large number of students. In 1920 they founded the journal *Fundamenta Mathematicae* (Fundamentals of mathematics) to publish papers in set theory, the area of the discipline in which they decided to concentrate their national research efforts. Under Sierpiński's leadership as editor in chief from 1920 to 1952, this periodical—the first mathematical journal to specialize in one area of the discipline—published research papers from international contributors and became one of the leading journals for the publication of research on set theory.

Sierpiński helped the Polish school of mathematics flourish in Warsaw and extend to other parts of the country. In 1921 he was elected a member of the Polish Academy of Sciences. Seven years later he became vice chairman of the Warsaw Scientific Society and chairman of the Polish Mathematical Society. In 1929, as chair of the Congress of Mathematicians of Slavic Countries, he helped bring together mathematicians from Poland and neighboring countries at an international conference in Warsaw. During the same year he participated in the establishment of a second mathematical research center in Lwów and another specialized journal, *Studia Mathematica* (Mathematical studies), which concentrated on the area of functional analysis. In 1932 he became the first editor of *Monografie Matematyczne* (Mathematical monographs), a series of advanced books on selected topics.

The outbreak of World War II in 1939 presented additional challenges to Sierpiński and his colleagues. He joined other members of the unofficial "Underground Warsaw University," holding forbidden classes at secret locations, including his own home. Although the war forced the suspension of the publication of Polish mathematical journals, he sent his research results to Italian journals, ending each paper with a promise that the proofs of the theorems would appear in *Fundamenta Mathematicae* after the war. During an uprising in 1944, the Nazis burned Sierpiński's home, destroyed his personal library, and imprisoned him near Kraków. When Allied military forces liberated the city later that year, Sierpiński lectured at Jagiellonian University before returning to Warsaw the following year. Although more than 50 percent of mathematicians from Polish universities died during the war, the Polish school reestablished itself with the creation in 1948 of the Institute of Mathematics in the Polish Academy of Sciences and the founding of new journals and publications.

During the three decades from 1918 to 1948, Sierpiński published hundreds of papers and books on set theory and topology. He wrote extensively on Cantor's continuum hypothesis that asserted there were no sizes of infinity between $\aleph_0$ (aleph-zero), the cardinality of the natural numbers, and $\aleph_1$ (aleph-one), the cardinality of the real numbers. In his 1934 book *Hypothèse du continu* (Continuum hypothesis) that appeared in the series *Monografie Matematyczne*, he investigated properties of topological spaces that would hold if the continuum hypothesis were true and would fail if it were false. In his 1945 paper "Sur un espace mètrique séparable universel" (On a universal, separable metric space), which appeared in *Fundamenta Mathematicae*, he proved that if the continuum hypothesis was true, a metric space with cardinality $\aleph_1$ that was universal would exist. Sierpiński proved that every metric space, with cardinality $\aleph_1$ would be identical to some subset of this universal space. In his 1947 paper "L'hypothèse généralisée du continu et l'axiome du choix" (The generalized continuum hypothesis and the axiom of choice), also published in *Fundamenta Mathematicae*, he showed that the axiom of choice could be proven from the continuum hypothesis and the 10 axioms of set theory.

Sierpiński's papers on topology focused primarily on metric spaces, collections of objects for which the distance between any two elements was well defined. Working with linear sets that are sets of real numbers and plane sets that are collections of ordered pairs of real numbers, he proved theorems about the properties of normality, separability, regularity, compactness, completeness, and connectedness. Typical of his results was his 1945 paper "Sur deux consequences d'un theoreme de Hausdorff" (On two consequences of a theorem by Hausdorff), which appeared in *Fundamenta Mathematicae*, in which he showed how to express the set of all real numbers as a sum of $\aleph_1$ disjoint infinite sets.

In his honor, topologists have assigned the name Sierpiński space to the topological space composed of two points denoted a and b and having the empty set, the set $\{a\}$, and the entire set $\{a, b\}$ as its three open sets. This simplest, nontrivial example of a topological space has important relations to the theory of computation and semantics.

Further Research in Number Theory

Between 1948 and 1968 Sierpiński wrote 11 books and more than 100 papers in number theory. His research addressed a wide variety of topics, employed diverse techniques, and introduced several innovations. In 1948 his paper "Remarque sur une hypothèse des Chinois concernant les nombres $(2^n - 2)/n$" (Remarks on a hypothesis by Chinois concerning the numbers $(2^n - 2)/n$) appeared in *Colloquium Mathematicum* (Mathematical colloquium), one of the newly founded publications of the Institute of Mathematics. The article investigated pseudoprimes, nonprime positive integers n that divide $2^n - 2$ without a remainder. Although the only pseudoprimes less than 1,000 are 341, 561, and 645, he proved that there are infinitely many such numbers by showing that whenever n is a pseudoprime, so is $2^n - 1$.

In several of his books and papers, Sierpiński presented unsolved or open problems in number theory to stimulate research on the topics. In his 1956 paper "Sur les décompositions de nombres rationels en fractions primaires" (On decompositions of rational numbers into unit fractions), which appeared in the French journal *Mathesis* (Mathematical papers), he challenged readers to prove the Sierpiński conjecture that the equation $\dfrac{5}{n} = \dfrac{1}{x} + \dfrac{1}{y} + \dfrac{1}{z}$ has integer solutions x, y, z for all positive integers n. His books *O stu protych ale trudnych zagadnieniach arytmetyki. Z pogranicza geometrii i arytmetyki* (One hundred elementary but difficult problems in arithmetic. On the borders of geometry and arithmetic), published in 1959, and *200 zadań z elementarnej teorii liczb* (Two hundred problems in elementary number theory), published in 1964, presented collections of open problems to engage amateurs, students, and professional mathematicians.

In 1958 he revisited the subject of relationships between circles and integer lattice points, the topic of his prize-winning paper from his student years. His paper "Sur quelques problèmes concernant les points aux coordonnées entières" (On several problems concerning points with integer coordinates) appearing in *L'Enseignement mathématique* (Mathematics education) provided a formula for the number of points with integer coordinates that could lie on the circumference of a circle. His 1959 paper "Sur les ensembles de points aux distances rationelles situés sur un cercle" (On sets of points at rational distances situated on a circle), which was published in the Swiss journal *Elemente der Mathematik* (Elements of mathematics), extended his analysis to circles having fractional radii.

Sierpiński introduced a new class of prime numbers that are known as Sierpiński numbers of the first kind in his 1958 paper "Sur les nombres premiers de la forme $n^n + 1$" (On prime numbers of the form $n^n + 1$) published in *L'Enseignement mathématique*. Sierpiński proved that if $n > 1$ and $n^n + 1$ is prime, then n must be of the form 2^{2^k}. Almost 50 years after he directed the attention of researchers to prime numbers of the form $n^n + 1$, the only known prime Sierpiński numbers of the first kind are 2, 5, and 257.

In 1958, when the Institute of Mathematics founded the journal *Acta Arithmetica* (Arithmetical activities) to provide a forum where Polish number theorists could publish their research results, Sierpiński became the publication's first editor in chief. His 1959 paper "Sur les nombres premiers ayant des chiffres initiaux et finals donnés" (On the prime numbers having given initial and final digits) appeared in this journal and presented a new property about the digits of prime numbers. His paper showed that for any two positive integers j and k and any sequences of digits $a_1 a_2 \, a_3 \cdots a_j$ and $b_1 b_2 \, b_3 \cdots b_k$ there was at least one prime number having the a's as its initial digits and the b's as its final digits provided the last digit was 1, 3, 7, or 9.

Although he retired from the University of Warsaw in 1960, at the age of 78, Sierpiński continued to conduct a seminar on number theory at the Polish Academy of Sciences until 1967 and remained an active contributor of new number theoretic ideas. He introduced the Sierpiński composite number theorem in his 1960 paper "Sur un problème concernant les nombres $k \cdot 2^n + 1$" (On a problem concerning the numbers $k \cdot 2^n + 1$), published in *Elemente der Mathematik*. In this paper he proved that there are infinitely many odd, positive integers k for which $k \cdot 2^n + 1$ is composite (nonprime) for all positive integers n. A number k having this property became known as a Sierpiński number of the second kind. In 1962 American mathematician John Selfridge proved that 78,557 was a Sierpiński number of the second kind and conjectured that it was the smallest number having the required properties. During the next 40 years researchers working on this conjecture, determined that all sequences of the form $k \cdot 2^n + 1$ based on smaller values of k contained at least one prime number with the exception of 17 specific values of k. In 2002 a group of mathematicians and computer scientists initiated a distributed computer project known as "Seventeen or Bust" with the aim of resolving the open question. By early 2006 they had eliminated nine of the 17 candidates, reducing to eight the number of possible Sierpiński numbers of the second kind that are smaller than 78,557.

Throughout his career Sierpiński wrote many papers about special classes of integers known as triangular numbers, pentagonal numbers, and tetrahedral numbers—integer quantities that can be arranged into particular geometrical patterns. He published two of these results in the journal *Elemente der Mathematik*. In a 1962 paper titled "Sur une propriété des nombres tétraédraux" (On a property of tetrahedral numbers), he proved that there are infinitely many positive integers x, y, and z that satisfy the equation $\binom{x}{3} + \binom{y}{3} = \binom{z}{3}$, where the notation $\binom{n}{3}$ represents the binominal coefficient $\dfrac{n \cdot (n-1) \cdot (n-2)}{3 \cdot 2 \cdot 1}$. In his 1963 paper titled "Trois nombres tétraédraux en progression arithmétique" (Three tetrahedral numbers in arithmetic progression), he proved that the equation $\binom{x}{3} + \binom{y}{3} = 2 \cdot \binom{z}{3}$ also had infinitely many positive integers solutions. He was able to show that the solutions $x = 10$, $y = 15$, $z = 17$ for the first equation and $x = 6$, $y = 12$, $z = 10$ for the second equation were only the simplest of infinitely many solutions of these diophantine equations.

In one of his final papers Sierpiński introduced a property that became known as the Sierpiński prime sequence theorem. His 1964 paper "Les binômes $x^2 + n$ et les nombres premiers" (The binomials $x^2 + n$ and prime numbers), which appeared in the *Bulletin de la Société Royale des Sciences Liège* (Bulletin of the Royal Society of Sciences at Liege), presented his proof that for every pair of positive integers n and k, the sequence $1^2 + n$, $2^2 + n$, $3^2 + n$, $4^2 + n, \cdots$ contains at least k prime numbers.

In addition to his research papers and his problem books, Sierpiński wrote nine books on number theory between 1955 and 1964. His 1955 textbook, *Arytmetyka teoretyczna* (The foundations of arithmetic), contained an exposition of elements of number theory. As a second volume to his work from 1911, he wrote *Teoria liczb II* (The theory of numbers, part II) in 1959. In 1964 he produced an expanded English edition titled *Elementary Theory of Numbers*. For more general audiences he produced six popular monographs on Pythagorean triangles, diophantine equations, sums of unit fractions, prime numbers, triangular number, and elementary aspects of number theory.

Sierpiński died on October 21, 1969, in Warsaw, at the age of 87. The government of Poland had honored him in 1949 with the Scientific Prize (First Class) and in 1958 with the Grand Cross of the Order of Polonia Restituta, a civilian award for meritorious service to his country. During his lifetime the prolific and respected mathematician wrote 724 mathematical papers and 50 books, served on the editorial boards of five journals, received nine honorary degrees, and was elected to membership in 14 scientific societies.

Conclusion

As a researcher in number theory, Sierpiński discovered the first absolutely normal number, investigated many properties of prime numbers, and introduced Sierpiński numbers of the first and second kind. In set theory and topology, he discovered many properties of metric spaces that were consequences of the continuum hypothesis. The Sierpiński snowflake and the Sierpiński triangle provided early examples of fractal images. His work with research institutions, specialized journals, and professional societies helped to establish and sustain the Polish school of mathematics.

FURTHER READING

Drucker, Thomas. "Wacław Sierpiński, 1882–1969, Polish Topologist and Logician." In *Notable Mathematicians: From Ancient Times to the Present*, edited by Robyn V. Young, 441–442. Detroit, Mich.: Gale, 1998. Brief but informative profile of Sierpiński and his work.

Kuratowski, Kazimierz. "Sierpiński, Wacław." In *Dictionary of Scientific Biography*, Vol. 12, edited by Charles C. Gillispie, 426–427. New York: Scribner, 1972. Brief encyclopedic biography.

———. "Wacław Sierpiński (1882–1969)." *Acta Arithmetica* 21 (1972): 1–5. Biographical sketch from the journal's memorial tribute to its founder and first editor.

Kuzmanovich, Jim. "Polish School of Mathematics." Wake Forest University. Available online. URL: http://www.math.wfu.edu/~kuz/Stamps/PolishSchool/PolishSchool.htm. Accessed August 24, 2005. Originally published in the mathematical stamp journal *Philmath*, this article presents a historical account of the Polish school of mathematics, with stamps and short biographical sketches of its leading figures.

O'Connor, J. J., and E. F. Robertson. "Wacław Sierpiński." MacTutor History of Mathematics Archive, University of Saint Andrews. Available online. URL: http://www-groups.dcs.st-andrews.ac.uk/~history/Mathematicians/Sierpiński.html. Accessed March 17, 2003. Online biography from the University of Saint Andrews, Scotland.

Schinzel, A. "Wacław Sierpiński's Papers on the Theory of Numbers." *Acta Arithmetica* 21 (1972): 7–13. Review of his work in number theory, part of the journal's memorial tribute to its founder and first editor.

"Wacław Sierpiński." Wikipedia: The Free Encyclopedia. Available online. URL: http://en.wikipedia.org/wiki/Sierpiński. Accessed August 22, 2005. Online biography with many related links.

Amalie Emmy Noether

4

(1882–1935)

Amalie Emmy Noether established the mathematical basis for Einstein's theory of relativity and developed methods that showed the importance of studying abstract algebraic structures. *(The Granger Collection)*

Abstract Algebraist

Amalie Emmy Noether (pronounced NER-thur) developed significant mathematical ideas in the theories of invariants, ideals, and noncommutative algebras. Noether's theorem about continuous symmetries and conserved quantities established the mathematical basis for Albert Einstein's theory of relativity. Her techniques and results on rings, ideals, and noncommutative algebras emphasized the importance of studying abstract algebraic structures. Through the Noether school, the informal group of researchers who conducted research with her, her ideas changed the way mathematicians worked in the field of algebra.

Early Years

Amalie Emmy Noether was born on March 23, 1882, in the town of Erlangen in the Bavarian region of southern Germany. Max Noether, her father, who held a position as a professor of mathematics at Erlangen University, was well known throughout the German mathematical community for his work in the field of algebra. Ida Amalia Kaufmann, her mother, was a talented pianist. All four Noether children—Emmy and her younger brothers Alfred, Fritz, and Gustav—obtained college educations. Three of the four earned doctoral degrees—Alfred in chemistry and Fritz and Emmy in mathematics.

From 1889 to 1897 Noether attended Städtische Höhere Töchterschule, the local public school for girls, where the curriculum emphasized languages, literature, and the arts, with limited exposure to science and mathematics. At the age of 18, after completing three years at a finishing school, she passed the examinations to obtain her certificate to teach French and English at girls' schools. She wanted to continue her education, but most German universities did not allow women to enroll as students. Only under exceptional circumstances and with the permission of individual professors could women attend lectures as auditors, but they could not take final exams or earn course credits.

In the winter semester of 1900–01, Noether obtained permission to audit courses in language, history, and mathematics at Erlangen University and became one of only two women studying with 984 men. Although her preparation was not as strong as her classmates' backgrounds, she excelled in mathematics and focused her studies in that area for the next three years. In 1903 she passed the *Reifeprüfung*, the national graduation examination that entitled her to enter any German university. She spent the winter semester of 1903–04 auditing mathematics courses at the University of Göttingen, where her professors included David Hilbert and Felix Klein, two of the best mathematicians in Europe. When Erlangen University changed its policies to admit female students in 1904, Noether enrolled as a full-time student majoring in mathematics.

For four years Noether took advanced mathematics courses at Erlangen University and conducted research with professor Paul

Gordan. Under his guidance she discovered new properties of ternary biquadratic forms, algebraic operators related to polynomials with three variables in which the exponents in every term add up to four, such as $f(x, y, z) = x^3y + 6y^2z^2 - 5xyz^2 + 7z^4$. Noether explained her research results in her dissertation, titled "Über die Bildung des Formensystems der ternären biquadratischen Form" (On the construction of the system of forms for the ternary biquadratic form). Her research results were announced in 1907 in the publication *Sitzung Berichten der Physikalisch-medizinische Sozietät in Erlangen* (Conference reports of the Society for Physics and Medicine in Erlangen). A formal paper with the same title providing a detailed explanation of her work appeared in 1908 in the *Journal für die reine und angewandte Mathematik* (Journal for pure and applied mathematics). This 67-page paper included a complete list of the 331 covariant forms that could be related to a single such polynomial. On December 13, 1907, she defended her thesis before a committee of mathematics professors, and at graduation ceremonies at the end of the spring semester, 26-year-old Noether received her doctorate in mathematics summa cum laude (with highest honors).

Invariant Theory

After becoming one of the first German women to earn a Ph.D. in any subject, Noether was unable to secure a faculty position at a German university. From 1908 to 1915 she worked as an informal, unpaid member of the mathematics department at Erlangen University, where she discussed mathematics with members of the faculty, continued her research, and taught her father's classes when he was ill. Although not an official faculty member, she served as research adviser for two students, Hans Falckenberg and Fritz Seidelmann, who earned their doctorates under her direction.

Noether became an active member of the European mathematical community, joining two professional mathematical societies—the Deutsche Mathematiker-Vereinigung (DMV; Association of German Mathematicians) and Circolo matematico di Palerma (Mathematical Circle of Palermo)—and frequently traveling to their conferences throughout Europe. In 1909 she presented her paper "Zur Invariantentheorie der Formen von n Variabeln" (On the theory of invariants for forms of n variables) at the DMV conference in Salzburg, Austria. An abbreviated summary of her work appeared in 1910 in the journal *Berichten der Deutsche Mathematiker-Vereinigung* (Conference reports of the Association of German Mathematicians). A more complete account appeared in a paper of the same name in 1911 in the *Journal für die reine und angewandte Mathematik*. In 1913 she presented yet another paper, titled "Rationale Funktionenkörper" (Fields of rational functions), at the DMV conference in Vienna, Austria. An extended report on this research, titled "Körper und Systeme rationaler Funktionen" (Fields and systems of rational functions), appeared two years later in the journal *Mathematische Annalen* (Annals of Mathematics). These two research papers along with her doctoral dissertation established Noether's reputation in the area of mathematics known as invariant theory, in which researchers study properties that remain fixed when an object is subjected to modifying transformations.

In 1915 Hilbert and Klein invited their former student to join their research group at the University of Göttingen where they were conducting research on applications of invariant theory. Albert Einstein, a physics professor at the University of Berlin, had formulated a general theory of relativity that explained the principles of gravity and motion in accelerated frames of reference. Hilbert and Klein were trying to determine the field equations for general relativity to describe the properties of a gravitational field surrounding a given mass.

During the next four years Noether produced nine research papers on various aspects of invariant theory. One early paper, "Gleichungen mit vorgeschriebener Gruppe" (Equations with pre-assigned group), written in 1916 and published two years later in *Mathematische Annalen*, determined the conditions under which a given group would be the Galois group of some polynomial equation. Her work represented the most significant contribution to the solution of this classic problem at the time.

Noether's landmark 1918 paper "Invariante variationsprobleme" (Invariant variational problems), published in *Nachrichten von der Gesellschaft der Wissenschaften zu Göttingen* (Report of the Society for the Sciences at Göttingen), was a major result in invariant theory. In this paper she proved a pair of theorems and their converses that are today collectively referred to as Noether's theorem. Working with finite and infinite symmetry groups, she determined the conditions under which symmetries of a group action corresponded to conserved quantities of a physical system. Because the principle of conservation of energy and momentum is a special case of these general results, Noether's theorem forms one of the cornerstones of the theory of general relativity. Her work provided the rigorous mathematical basis for Einstein's theory. This result has become a basic tool in quantum field theory and particle physics.

Struggle for Faculty Appointment

From the time that Noether first came to Göttingen, Hilbert and Klein had tried to obtain for her an official appointment to the university's faculty. In 1915, as part of the formal process of qualifying for *Habilitation* (lectureship), Noether presented the paper "Über ganze transzendentte Zahlen" (On transcendental integers) to the Mathematical Society in Göttingen. At a subsequent meeting of the faculty, some professors argued to maintain the rule that prohibited women from joining the faculty, asserting that it would be humiliating to require male students to learn from female professors. Hilbert angrily replied that it should make no difference whether a professor was a man or a woman because this was a university, not a bathhouse. Although his passionate plea did not change his colleagues' minds, he did obtain permission from the government's minister of education to allow Noether to teach some of his classes as his unpaid assistant.

In 1919, when the post–World War I German government relaxed many restrictions, Noether presented her paper "Invariante variationsprobleme" as her *Habilitation* thesis and obtained an appointment to the faculty at the lowest possible rank. Her title of *Privatdozent* (assistant professor) permitted her to officially teach courses at the university under her own name but without any pay. Three years later the university awarded her the higher faculty rank of *ausserordentlicher Professor* (untenured associate professor) but did not provide her a salary. In 1923 her mathematical colleagues secured for her an official *Lehrauftrag* (commission to teach) that paid her a small salary, although her contract had to be renewed every year.

With little or no financial support from the university, Noether lived a modest lifestyle maintained by a small inheritance from her mother and father, who had both died since she had come to Göttingen, and by money that two of her uncles sent on a regular basis. Dressing plainly and eating simply, she enjoyed cooking dinner at her apartment for "the Noether boys," a group of devoted students who were attracted by her friendly personality and her mathematical brilliance. In her years at Göttingen, she directed the thesis research of 10 Noether boys who earned their Ph.D.s, and she continued to help many of them with their later research papers.

Ideal Theory

From 1920 to 1926 Noether focused her work on a branch of abstract algebra known as ideal theory. Her work in this area profoundly changed the emphasis of research in algebra by focusing attention on abstract properties of structures called groups, rings, fields, ideals, and modules rather than on the specific objects themselves. She introduced this radical approach to studying algebraic structures in her 1920 paper "Modulen in nichtkommutativen Bereichen, insbesondere aus Differential- und Differenzenausdrücken" (Modules in noncommutative domains, in particular in differential and difference equations), written in collaboration with W. Schmeidler and published in *Mathematische Zeitschrift* (Mathematical reviews). In the context of rings of differential operators, this paper also introduced the concepts of left and right ideals.

Noether's 1921 paper "Idelatheorie in Ringbereichen" (Theory of ideals in ring domains), published in *Mathematische Annalen*, presented her most important results in ideal theory. In this paper she proved that for a commutative ring with an ideal, the ascending chain condition was equivalent to the condition that every ideal have a finite basis and to the condition that every set of ideals have a maximal element. Because of the significance of the results obtained and the wide applicability of the techniques used, this paper laid the foundation for modern abstract algebra. With concepts that came to be known as Noetherian rings and Noetherian ideals, this and subsequent papers revolutionized the study of abstract algebra.

Noether published 15 papers on ideal theory and presented six of them at meetings of the DMV. The publications included the 1923 paper "Eliminationstheorie und allgemeine Idealtheorie" (Elimination theory and the general theory of ideals) and the 1927 paper "Abstrakter Aufbau der Idealtheorie in algebraischen Zahl- und Funcktionenkörpern" (Abstract structures of ideal theory in algebraic

$$(1) = \{...,-3, -2, -1, 0, 1, 2, 3, ...\}$$
$$\cup I$$
$$(2) = \{...,-6, -4, -2, 0, 2, 4, 6, ...\}$$
$$\cup I$$
$$(4) = \{...,-12, -8, -4, 0, 4, 8, 12, ...\}$$
$$\cup I$$
$$(20) = \{...,-60, -40, -20, 0, 20, 40, 60, ...\}$$
$$\cup I$$
$$(100) = \{...,-300, -200, -100, 0, 100, 200, 300, ...\}$$

$$(100) \triangleleft (20) \triangleleft (4) \triangleleft (2) \triangleleft (1)$$

© Infobase Publishing

In the ring of integers, all the multiples of an integer n form an ideal that is denoted (n). The multiples of 20 form a subset of the multiples of 4, which in turn form a subset of the multiples of 2. Since any such chain of ideals must have a last member, the integers satisfy the ascending chain condition.

number and function fields), both published in *Mathematische Annalen*. Her conference papers included the 1925 paper "Hillbertsche Anzahlen in der Idealtheorie" (Hilbert numbers in the theory of ideals) and the 1926 report "Gruppencharaktere und Idealtheorie" (Group characters and the theory of ideals). These papers demonstrated the wide applicability of the concepts she introduced.

International Influence

During the 1920s Noether gathered around herself an excellent group of students and professors who worked together on research in abstract algebra. The Mathematical Institute at the University of Göttingen became the center of mathematical research in the world, and her research group, informally known as the Noether school, earned a reputation as the most talented, productive, and influential group at the institute. Mathematicians came to Göttingen from every country in Europe as well as from Japan, Russia, and the United States to conduct research with her. When these professors returned to their universities, they shared her ideas on abstract algebraic structures with their colleagues, enabling Noether's ideas to have a profound influence on mathematics internationally.

As an unpaid editor of the journal *Mathematische Annalen*, Noether reviewed the research papers submitted by many mathematicians and suggested corrections, revisions, and related problems for consideration. Although she published 43 research papers in mathematical journals, she allowed other mathematicians and students to take credit for many ideas that she had developed during her class lectures and in the meetings of her research group. Noether's innovative ideas significantly changed the way researchers conducted research in algebra and in many other branches of mathematics. Her theories enabled mathematicians to make important and fundamental discoveries in algebraic geometry and algebraic topology, as well as in physics and chemistry, by studying the abstract structure of similar collections of objects. Her ideas influenced the teaching of mathematics in U.S. elementary schools 50 years later in the form of the "New Math" of the 1970s.

Noncommutative Algebras

From 1927 to 1935 Noether redirected the focus of her research to study noncommutative algebras, algebraic structures in which two objects combined in one order produce different results than the same two objects combined in the opposite order. She studied rings of matrices and functions, linear transformations, hypercomplex numbers, cross-products, and other noncommutative objects. Her research on noncommutative algebras employed the same high level of abstract analysis as her work on ideals, enabling her to prove deep and powerful theorems.

During this period of years Noether published 13 papers on noncommutative algebras, three of which were particularly influential. Her 1929 paper "Hyperkomplexe Grossen und Darstellungstheorie" (Hypercomplex quantities and representation theory), presented at a conference in Bologna, Italy, and published in *Mathematische Zeitschrift*, introduced the fundamental ideas of noncommutative algebras. In her 1933 paper "Nichtkommutative Algebren" (Noncommutative algebras), published in *Mathematische Zeitschrift*, she more fully explained the general theory of the subject. The 1932 paper "Beweis eines Hauptsatzes in der Theorie for Algebren" (Proof of a main theorem in the theory of algebras), which she jointly wrote with German mathematicians Richard Brauer and Helmut Hasse, proved the fundamental result that every simple algebra over an ordinary algebraic number field is cyclic. German algebraist Herman Weyl regarded this paper as a high-water mark in the development of algebra.

Honors and Recognitions

Noether's reputation within the larger mathematical community enabled her to undertake a variety of projects. She spent the 1928–29 academic year as a visiting professor at Moscow University in Russia, teaching a course in abstract algebra and collaborating with Pavel Alexandrov and other researchers. During the summer of 1930 she taught as a visiting professor at Frankfurt University. With German mathematician Robert Fricke and the Norwegian mathematician Øystein Ore, she edited the *Collected Mathematical Works* of Richard Dedekind, published in three volumes between 1930 and 1932. In the third volume, her detailed commentaries on the German mathematician's works were so thorough that they were reprinted in 1964 as a separate book titled *Über die Theorie der ganzsen algebraischen Zahlen* (On the theory of algebraic integers). She also worked with French mathematician Jean Cavaillès to edit the correspondence between Russian mathematician Georg Cantor and Dedekind. Completed in 1933 this work was published four years later in *Actualités scientifiques et industrielles* (Scientific and industrial news).

Two events in 1932 indicated the stature and reputation Noether had achieved within the mathematical community. Along with Austrian algebraist Emil Artin, she was awarded the Alfred Ackermann-Taubner Memorial Award for the advancement of the mathematical sciences. Although the monetary value of the prestigious award was only 500 marks (about $120), it affirmed her colleagues' high regard for the quality of her research, the importance of her publications, and her knowledge of her discipline. In September she was invited to deliver one of the main addresses at the International Mathematical Congress in Switzerland. Her conference paper, "Hypercomplexe Systeme in ihren Beziehungen zur kommutativen Algebra und zur Zahlentheorie" (Hypercomplex systems in their relations to commutative algebra and to number theory), was well received by the 800 mathematicians in attendance.

Last Years in America

Noether's productive career was interrupted in 1933 when Adolf Hitler, the new German chancellor, instituted a series of laws that barred Jews from leadership positions within German society. In April the Prussian Ministry of Science, Art, and Public Education notified Noether that they had withdrawn her permission to teach at the University of Göttingen. She continued to meet with her students and with her research group at her apartment while trying to secure an academic position in Russia, Britain, or the United States. By October, with the help of the Rockefeller Foundation and the Emergency Committee to Aid Displaced German Scholars, she obtained an appointment at Bryn Mawr College, a premier women's college in Pennsylvania.

Noether made a rapid transition into the American mathematical community. Her colleagues at Bryn Mawr included department chair Anna Pell Wheeler, one of the best-known female mathematicians in the United States, and Olga Tausky-Todd, a postgraduate fellow who later became the first female professor at the California Institute of Technology. Both women had studied at the University of Göttingen and were familiar with German culture. Noether taught seminars in algebra, attracted a small following of ambitious students, and directed the Ph.D. thesis of one student, Ruth Stauffer. Each week Noether visited the Institute for Advanced Study in Princeton, New Jersey, where she gave lectures and collaborated on research projects with other mathematicians, including many who, like herself, had been forced to leave Germany. Her only research paper written in America, "Zerfallende verschränkte Produckte und ihre Maximalordnungen" (Splitting crossed products and their maximal orders), appeared in 1934 in *Actualités scientifiques et industrielles*.

In April 1935 doctors removed a large cancerous tumor from Noether's abdomen. Four days later, on April 14, she died at the age of 53. In the months following her unexpected death, Noether's international mathematical colleagues paid tribute to her. The mathematics journal *Mathematische Annalen*, which had never listed her name as one of their editors, defied the German government by publishing a lengthy article praising her life and her work. The Moscow Mathematical Society organized a conference in her honor at which mathematicians from around the world gave speeches about her life and presented papers about her research. The *New York Times* published a letter signed by Einstein in which he called Noether the greatest woman mathematician who had ever lived.

Conclusion

Despite societal prejudices against women and Jews, Noether became an accomplished mathematician and made significant discoveries in physics and mathematics. Noether's theorem rigorously established the mathematical basis for Einstein's theory of relativity and has become a fundamental tool in quantum field theory and particle physics. She wrote numerous important research papers in ideal theory and the theory of noncommutative algebras. As the leader of the Noether school, she demonstrated the benefits of studying the abstract structure of collections of mathematical objects, changing the way that mathematicians conduct research in the field of algebra.

FURTHER READING

Byers, Nina. "Emmy Noether." Contributions of 20th Century Women in Physics, University of California at Los Angeles. Available online. URL: http://cwp.library.ucla.edu/Phase2/ Noether,_Amalie_Emmy@861234567.html. Accessed August 3, 2005. Biographical sketch with a link to a reprint of the paper "E. Noether's Discovery of the Deep Connection between Symmetries and Conservation Laws," given at a 1996 conference by Dr. Byers of the Department of Physics at UCLA.

Crawford, Mary. "Emmy Noether: She Did Einstein's Math." *Ms.* 10 (1981): 86–89. Magazine article providing some biographical information and a description of selected work.

Dick, Auguste. *Emmy Noether, 1882–1935.* Boston: Birkhauser, 1981. H. L. Blocher's English translation of the authoritative German book-length biography.

Hall, Loretta. "Emmy Noether, 1882–1935, German-Born American Algebraist and Educator." In *Notable Mathematicians: From Ancient Times to the Present,* edited by Robyn V. Young, 372–375. Detroit, Mich.: Gale, 1998. Brief but informative profile of Noether and her work.

Henderson, Harry. "Emmy Noether (1882–1935)." In *Modern Mathematicians,* 46–57. New York: Facts On File, 1996. Biographical profile.

James, Ioan. "Emmy Noether." In *Remarkable Mathematicians from Euler to von Neumann,* 321–326. Washington, D.C.: Mathematical Association of America, 2003. Brief biography and description of her mathematics.

Kimberling, Clark H. "Emmy Noether." *American Mathematical Monthly* 79 (1972): 136–149. Article in mathematics journal providing a detailed description of her work with some biographical information.

———. "Emmy Noether, Greatest Woman Mathematician." *Mathematics Teacher* 84, no. 3 (1982): 246–249. Article in mathematics education journal providing a description of her work with some biographical information.

Kramer, Edna E. "Noether, Amalie Emmy." In *Dictionary of Scientific Biography*, Vol. 10, edited by Charles C. Gillispie, 137–139. New York: Scribner, 1972. Encyclopedic biography, including a detailed description of her mathematical writings.

Morrow, James. "Emmy Noether." In *Notable Women in Mathematics: A Biographical Dictionary*, edited by Charlene Morrow and Teri Perl, 152–157. Westport, Conn.: Greenwood Press, 1998. Short biography.

Noether, Gottfried E. "Emmy Noether (1882–1935)." In *Women of Mathematics: A Biobibliographic Sourcebook*, edited by Louise S. Grinstein and Paul J. Campbell, 165–170. New York: Greenwood Press, 1987. Biographical profile with discussion of her work.

O'Connor, J. J., and E. F. Robertson. "Emmy Amalie Noether." MacTutor History of Mathematics Archive, University of Saint Andrews. Available online. URL: http://www-groups.dcs.st-andrews.ac.uk/~history/Mathematicians/Noether_Emmy.html. Accessed August 1, 2003. Biography from the University of Saint Andrews, Scotland.

Osen, Lynn M. "Emmy (Amalie) Noether." In *Women in Mathematics*, 141–152. Cambridge, Mass.: MIT Press, 1974. Biographical sketch of Noether and her work.

Perl, Teri. "Emmy Noether." In *Math Equals: Biographies of Women Mathematicians + Related Activities*, 172–194. Menlo Park, Calif.: Addison-Wesley, 1978. Biography accompanied by exercises related to her mathematical work.

Reimer, Luetta, and Wilbert Reimer. "Life on an Obstacle Course: Emmy Noether." In *Mathematicians Are People, Too: Stories from the Lives of Great Mathematicians*, 114–121. Parsippany, N.J.: Seymour, 1990. Life story with historical facts and fictionalized dialogue; intended for elementary school students.

5

Srinivasa Iyengar Ramanujan

(1887–1920)

Self-taught number theorist Srinivasa Iyengar Ramanujan developed techniques for approximating the constant π, analyzing highly composite numbers, and determining the number of ways to partition a given integer. *(The Granger Collection)*

Indian Number Theorist

Working in isolation for most of his life, Srinivasa Iyengar Ramanujan (pronounced shreen-ee-VAH-sah eye-YEN-gahr rah-MAH-noo-jah) developed thousands of theorems about infinite series and the properties of positive integers. During a five-year stay in England, he published papers on techniques for approximating the constant π, the analysis of highly composite numbers, the number of prime factors of a positive integer, and the number of ways to partition a given integer. His innovative methods for investigating these and other topics in number theory contributed to the development of probabilistic and additive number theory. Mathematicians continue to study the mock theta functions he introduced as well as the contents of the notebooks where he recorded his discoveries.

Societal Influences

Srinivasa Iyengar Ramanujan was born on December 22, 1887, at his grandmother's house in the town of Erode in the Madras province of southern India. A year later his family moved 100 miles north to the city of Kumbakonam. Srinivasa, his father, worked as a clerk for a cloth merchant, earning a meager salary of 20 rupees a month. Komalatammal, his mother, supplemented the family's income by singing devotional songs at a nearby temple. As the oldest of six children, three of whom died as infants, he was the focus of his mother's attention and affection.

Ramanujan and his family belonged to the Brahmin caste and were devoted followers of the Hindu religion. According to traditional Indian customs, Ramanujan took his father's name, Srinivasa, followed by the name his parents chose for him, Ramanujan, meaning "younger brother of Rama," the model of Indian manhood from the epic Indian tale the *Ramayana*. His middle name, Iyengar, indicated the subsect of the caste of Brahmins to which his family belonged. Although most of India's priests, scholars, and religious leaders came from this highest class, his family's financial situation prevented him from taking advantage of the opportunities available to Brahmins for education, career, marriage, and other aspects of life. Following the rules of the Brahmin caste, the family ate a strict vegetarian diet and carefully prepared their food according to specific guidelines. They prayed to many Hindu gods and goddesses at home and at shrines. Ramanujan and his mother developed a devotion to the goddess Namagiri, whom they believed to be his special protector.

In his appearance, Ramanujan was dark skinned and overweight. Although skin tones among Indians varied widely from fair to brown to black, his skin color was so dark that his university professors in England referred to him as a black man. In a country where many children were underfed and most residents were thin, Ramanujan's stout stature was due to his doting mother's insistence that her favorite child have plenty to eat and his preference for quiet games rather than sports and rugged activities.

Even though he did not speak until he was three years old, Ramanujan excelled in all his subjects when he attended Kangayan Primary School. At the age of nine, he earned the highest score in the Tanjore school district on the Primary Examination, a standardized test of English, arithmetic, geography, and his native Tamil language. The following year he earned a half-tuition scholarship and was admitted to "Form I," the equivalent of sixth grade, at Town High School, where his talent for mathematics became evident to both his teachers and his classmates. In the eighth grade his teacher presented the fundamental property of division that any number divided by itself is one by explaining that whether three fruits were divided equally among three people or 1,000 fruits were divided equally among 1,000 people, each person would get one piece of fruit. Yet, Ramanujan asked if zero divided by zero was also one; if there was no fruit and no people, would each person still get one? When he was 14, an older classmate challenged him to find two whole numbers x and y that satisfied the equations $\sqrt{x} + y = 7$ and $\sqrt{y} + x = 11$. After thinking for less than a minute, Ramanujan produced the answer $x = 9$, $y = 4$ and then explained how to solve the problem in two efficient steps.

Ramanujan's poor family was often unable to buy paper, pencils, or the textbooks that he needed for school. He did most of his calculations using chalk to write on a slate, a small piece of blackboard enclosed in a wooden frame. When he had filled his slate with numbers and had no more room to write, he would erase the figures by rubbing his elbow across them. He frequently borrowed books from the college students who rented rooms at his family's home. By the age of 13 he had mastered the mathematics in a borrowed copy of Sidney L. Loney's *Trigonometry* from which he learned that the sine and cosine of an angle could be calculated by adding up the terms of an infinite series rather than by dividing the lengths of the sides of a right triangle. Through independent investigations he developed the mathematical theory that explained the correspondence between the two approaches to trigonometric functions and showed his original analysis to his teacher. When his teacher explained that Swiss mathematician Leonhard Euler had made the same discovery 150 years earlier, Ramanujan was so embarrassed that he went home and hid the papers beneath the roof of his house.

Mathematics became Ramanujan's passion at the age of 15 when he borrowed a copy of George S. Carr's *Synopsis of Elementary Results in Pure and Applied Mathematics*. This large book contained thousands of mathematical rules from algebra, geometry, calculus, and differential equations without any proofs to explain why the statements were true. Ramanujan spent months working through the listing of theorems, formulas, and geometrical diagrams, developing his own style of reasoning to justify the validity of each result. Many times he would go to bed thinking of unsolved math problems and get up at night to write down ideas that had occurred to him while he slept.

During his high school years Ramanujan received many awards for excellence in mathematics and literature. He regularly won problem-solving competitions and ranked as the top student in mathematics each year. When headmaster Krishnaswami Iyer awarded him the K. Ranganatha Rao Prize for mathematics in 1904, he remarked that Ramanujan's work was so good that he deserved more than the maximum score of 100 points. In addition to his merit certificates for achievement in mathematics, he also received books of poetry for winning several English contests.

The Notebook Years, 1904–1914

During his final year of high school Ramanujan passed the Matriculation Examination of the University of Madras and won the Junior Subrahmanyan Scholarship for excellence in English and mathematics. In 1904, at the age of 16, he became a student at Government College in Kumbakonam. Dedicating his energies exclusively to the study of mathematics, he failed his other subjects, lost his scholarship, and ran away from home for three months. In 1906 he was admitted to Pachaiyappa's College in Madras where he excelled in mathematics but failed the fine arts exam twice and was dismissed from the college.

$$\frac{1}{n+1} + \frac{1}{n+2} + \frac{1}{n+3} + \frac{1}{n+4} + \ldots + \frac{1}{2n} = \frac{n}{2n+1} + \frac{1}{2^3-2} + \frac{1}{4^3-4} + \frac{1}{6^3-6} + \ldots + \frac{1}{(2n)^3-2n}$$

$$\text{For } n = 3, \quad \frac{1}{4} + \frac{1}{5} + \frac{1}{6} = \frac{3}{7} + \frac{1}{6} + \frac{1}{60} + \frac{1}{210}$$

In chapter 2 of his second notebook, Ramanujan recorded this summation formula followed by a brief proof. When n = 3 the formula becomes a simple equation in which both sides are equal to 37/60.

Although his intensive study of mathematics had resulted in his dismissal from two colleges, Ramanujan's independent investigations during those years had led him to discover new mathematical ideas. In three large notebooks he recorded theorems and formulas that did not appear in the books he had borrowed from libraries and professors. For several years he earned money as a tutor but spent most of his time studying mathematics and researching original ideas. In his notebooks he organized his discoveries into 38 chapters and numbered the theorems consecutively. The topics included methods for constructing magic squares, approximations for mathematical constants, properties of prime numbers, and techniques for analyzing infinite series, continued fractions, and infinite products. In 10 years he recorded more than 3,500 results in the 640 pages of his three notebooks.

In 1909 Ramanujan entered into an arranged marriage with Srimathi Janaki Ammal, his 10-year-old distant cousin. While his wife continued to live with her parents, Ramanujan traveled throughout southern India showing his notebooks to friends, mathematics professors at many colleges and universities, and the leaders of the Indian Mathematical Society. In 1911 Ramachandra Rao, district collector in the city of Nellore and secretary of the Indian Mathematical Society, supported him with a monthly stipend of 25 rupees so he could continue his research in Madras while seeking a more suitable position. The following year he obtained a job making 30 rupees per month as a clerk in the accounting department of the Madras Port Trust, the government office that managed the ship traffic in the harbor at Madras. Two of his supervisors were Narayana Iyer, the treasurer of the Indian Mathematical Society, and Sir Francis Spring, an English engineer who had high-ranking British contacts throughout India. Although neither man understood Ramanujan's work, both of them recognized his talent, encouraged him to keep working on his notebooks, helped him to submit his research results to mathematical journals, and tried to obtain a research fellowship for him at a university.

Between 1911 and 1913 the *Journal of the Indian Mathematical Society* published five pieces of Ramanujan's work. In his first paper, "Some Properties of Bernoulli's Numbers," he used the infinite series for the cotangent function to produce efficient methods for determining the values of Bernoulli's numbers, a sequence of fractions that occurred in many applications in number theory and analysis. His 1912 papers "On Question 330 of Professor Sanjana" and "Note on a Set of Simultaneous Equations" presented a method for summing a particular infinite series and a technique for solving a system of 10 equations with 10 unknowns. In his 1913 paper "Irregular Numbers" he gave several formulas involving the sequence of integers 2, 3, 5, 7, 8, 11, 12, 13, 17, 18, ... that have an odd number of prime factors and the sequence of integers 2, 3, 5, 6, 7, 10, 11, 13, 14, 15, ... that have no repeated prime factors. He used these sequences to determine values for infinite products such as $\left(1+\frac{1}{2^2}\right)\cdot\left(1+\frac{1}{3^2}\right)\cdot\left(1+\frac{1}{5^2}\right)\cdot\left(1+\frac{1}{7^2}\right)\cdots=\frac{15}{\pi^2}$ and for infinite sums such as $\frac{1}{2^2}+\frac{1}{3^2}+\frac{1}{5^2}+\frac{1}{6^2}+\cdots=\frac{\pi^2}{20}$. In the brief note "Squaring the Circle" that was published in 1913, he provided a simple method for constructing a line segment whose square produced an approximation for the area of a given circle. He noted that for a circle having an area of 140,000 square miles, the length of the segment constructed by his method differed by approximately an inch from the true length of the side of the square having the same area.

A regular feature of many mathematical periodicals was the publication of challenging problems submitted by readers. Between 1911 and 1919 the journal published 59 problems posed by Ramanujan, including nine in the first of these years. His collection of problems involved derivatives, integrals, infinite series, infinite products, simultaneous equations, perfect squares, and arithmetic identities. One of his questions asked readers to find pairs of positive rational numbers that satisfied the equation $x^y = y^x$, such as $x = 4$, $y = 2$ and $x = \dfrac{27}{8}$, $y = \dfrac{9}{4}$. Another problem requested a proof that every positive integer satisfied the identity $\lfloor \sqrt{n} + \sqrt{n+1} \rfloor = \lfloor \sqrt{4n+2} \rfloor$, where the symbol $\lfloor\ \rfloor$ indicated the greatest integer that was less than or equal to the expression inside the brackets. None of the journal's readers was able to answer his question that asked them to determine why the expression

$$\sqrt{1+2\sqrt{1+3\sqrt{1+4\sqrt{1+5\sqrt{1+6\sqrt{1+\cdots}}}}}}$$ was equal to 3.

In January 1913 Ramanujan sent a letter and 10 pages of formulas from his notebooks to Godfrey Hardy, one of the leading mathematicians at Cambridge University in England. When Hardy and his colleague John Littlewood reviewed the sample of Ramanujan's work, they discovered that although some of the formulas were incorrect and other results had been discovered previously, there were many profound and elegant formulas that hinted at his deep mathematical talent. Hardy talked excitedly to the other professors about the "new Euler" he had discovered in India and wrote back to Ramanujan, inviting him to come to England to work.

Although Ramanujan was pleased by Hardy's offer and understood the opportunity it offered to advance in his career, he declined. As a member of the Brahmin caste, he would be considered "unclean" if he traveled to a foreign country and would be "shunned," meaning he would no longer be allowed to be with his family or friends. Hardy's interest in supporting Ramanujan led officials at the University of Madras to appoint him as a special research scholar and award him a monthly stipend of 75 rupees beginning in May 1913. During his first 10 months as a professional mathematician, he continued his correspondence with Hardy, prepared several articles on his notebook results for publications, and submitted three reports to the university's Board of Studies in Mathematics on the progress of his research.

Four of Ramanujan's research articles from this period appeared in the 1915 volume of the *Journal of the Indian Mathematical Society.* "On the Number of Divisors of a Number" provided an upper limit for the number of positive integers that divide a given number without leaving a remainder. "On the Sum of the Square Roots of the First *n* Natural Numbers" presented formulas for sums such as

$1\sqrt{1} + 2\sqrt{2} + 3\sqrt{3} + \ldots + n\sqrt{n}$ and $\dfrac{1}{\sqrt{1}} + \dfrac{1}{\sqrt{2}} + \dfrac{1}{\sqrt{3}} + \ldots + \dfrac{1}{\sqrt{n}}$. The other

two papers analyzed an integral involving the arctangent function and an infinite product of fractions.

Late in December 1913, after Ramanujan spent three nights at the shrine of the goddess Namagiri in Namakkal, he decided to accept Hardy's invitation to study in England. When his mother had a dream in which Namagiri warned her not to interfere with her son's career, she gave her permission for him to travel. In February the University of Madras awarded him a two-year research stipend of £250 per year, plus traveling expenses. Hardy arranged for a full scholarship for Ramanujan to study at Cambridge University's Trinity College and an additional £60 stipend. He left India by boat in March and arrived in London a month later.

Years in England, 1914–1919

Ramanujan immediately started classes and began to work with Hardy and Littlewood. In his classes he extended his instructors' presentations to new theorems that they had not yet discovered. He explained to Hardy the unusual notations in his notebooks, shared the inspirations that had led him to his ideas, and revealed the techniques he had used to justify his results. Hardy showed Ramanujan how to write rigorous mathematical proofs. Littlewood taught him about doubly periodic functions, complex functions, and other topics that filled gaps in his uneven knowledge of mathematics. Neither professor was completely successful, because as soon as Ramanujan learned a new idea, his active mind thought of several more that took him in a different direction than his professors had intended to go. Sensitive to this tendency, Hardy tried not to destroy Ramanujan's creative genius by forcing him to think like other mathematicians. Together they prepared for publication the best results from his notebooks and started conducting research in new directions.

Ramanujan's first publication in a European mathematics journal, his 1914 paper "Modular Equations and Approximations to π," which appeared in the *Quarterly Journal of Mathematics*, presented a variety of methods for generating estimates for the value

of π. His simple calculations $\sqrt[4]{9^2 + \frac{19^2}{22}} = 3.1415926526 \dots$ and

$\frac{355}{113}\left(1 - \frac{.0003}{3533}\right) = 3.141592653589794\dots$ provided approximations

for the actual value of π = 3.141592653589798 . . . that were accurate to eight and 14 digits, respectively. Using logarithms and square roots, he produced additional estimates that were correct to as many as 31 decimal places. Among all the estimates he had discovered, the most original were the seven-digit approximation

$\frac{1}{2\sqrt{2}}\left(\frac{99^2}{1103}\right) = 3.14159273 \dots$ provided by a single term of an

infinite series and the nine-digit estimate $\frac{63}{25}\left(\frac{17+15\sqrt{5}}{7+15\sqrt{5}}\right) =$

3.1415926538 . . . given by the ratio to two surds, expressions of the form $a + b\sqrt{c}$, where a, b, and c are integers. This paper also provided new insights into the properties of elliptic and modular functions. Today, mathematicians working with computers continue to use some of the infinite series presented in this paper to calculate the digits of π.

At the June 1914 meeting of the London Mathematical Society, Hardy presented some of Ramanujan's results from number theory, the branch of mathematics dealing with properties of integers. The full text of Ramanujan's lengthy treatise on the topic, "Highly Composite Numbers," appeared in 1915 in the *Proceedings of the London Mathematical Society*. His work described highly composite numbers, positive integers having more factors than any smaller number. The first highly composite numbers are 2, 4, 6, 12, 24, and 36; they have 2, 3, 4, 6, 8, and 9 factors, respectively. Ramanujan provided upper and lower bounds for the value of the function $d(n)$

that specified the number of factors of the positive integer n. His analysis of the properties of this class of numbers demonstrated his mastery of the algebra of inequalities.

In less than two years, Ramanujan submitted his treatise on highly composite numbers and six other papers on various topics in number theory to the faculty at Trinity College. In March 1916 the institution awarded him a "Bachelor of Science by Research," which became known four years later as a doctor of philosophy, or Ph.D. The University of Madras extended its financial support of his work for an additional three years, during which time he published 15 more papers in his own name and an additional seven papers in collaboration with Hardy.

In 1917 Ramanujan and Hardy published a series of joint papers about prime numbers, whole numbers such as 2, 3, 5, 7, 11, 13, and 17 that are greater than one but cannot be divided by any other positive numbers except themselves and one. In their paper "The Normal Number of Prime Factors of a Number n," which appeared in the *Quarterly Journal of Mathematics*, they presented a formula that almost always gave the correct value for the number of primes that divided each positive integer n. By showing that a general positive integer n had about $\log(\log(n))$ prime factors, they demonstrated that round numbers—numbers having many prime factors—were very rare. This paper and the related papers they produced during that year presented the first systematic discussion of the number of prime divisors of a positive integer. During the next 30 years, other mathematicians built on their results and developed the branch of mathematics known as probabilistic number theory.

In a series of three papers published between 1916 and 1918, Ramanujan presented new ideas on the topic of representing numbers as the sum of squares. His 1916 paper "On Certain Arithmetical Functions" and his 1918 paper "On Certain Trigonometrical Sums and Their Applications in the Theory of Numbers," both of which appeared in the *Transactions of the Cambridge Philosophical Society*, introduced infinite series that provided estimates for important number theoretic functions such as $\sigma(n)$, the sum of the divisors of the positive integer n, and $\phi(n)$, the number of prime numbers less than n. In his 1917 paper "On the Expression of a Number in the Form $ax^2 + by^2 + cz^2 + dt^2$," published in the *Proceedings of the Cambridge Philosophical Society*, he proved that there were 55 sets of positive integers a, b, c, and d for which every positive integer could be expressed in the form $ax^2 + by^2 + cz^2 + dt^2$. His papers on the representation of numbers as sums of squares enabled other mathematicians to discover many new results in this area of classical number theory.

In his first letter to Hardy in 1913, Ramanujan had mentioned his analysis of partitions of positive integers, ways of expressing a number as a sum of positive integers. In a 1918 paper titled "Asymptotic Formulae in Combinatory Analysis" that appeared in the *Proceedings of the Cambridge Philosophical Society*, he and Hardy presented an asymptotic, or approximation, formula that came very close to giving the exact value of $p(n)$, the number of partitions of the positive integer n. By taking the sum of a specified number of terms of an infinite series and rounding off the decimal answer to the nearest integer, their formula produced the correct value of $p(n)$. In the next several years other mathematicians built on their ideas to discover an exact formula for $p(n)$ and developed their asymptotic approach into a formal method called the circle method that could be used to solve many problems in the field of additive number theory.

In the five years that Ramanujan worked with Hardy in England, they published 28 research papers in British mathematical journals. These papers made substantial contributions to number theory and to the analysis of elliptic functions, continued fractions, and infinite series. Their work led to major developments in many areas of mathematics. In recognition of Ramanujan's contribution to mathematics, he was elected a fellow of the London Mathematical Society, a fellow of Trinity College, and a fellow of the Royal Society of London. He was the first Indian and the first Asian to be honored by the Royal Society. In 1918 when he was elected to the Royal Society, only 15 of the 104 candidates who were nominated from all branches of science were chosen.

Although Ramanujan's years in England were productive mathematically, he suffered from physical and mental illnesses. Lonely for his wife, his mother, and his friends; bothered by the cold, damp climate of England; prevented from returning to India by World War I; and unable to cook the traditional foods for his Brahmin vegetarian diet, he became so depressed that he tried to commit suicide by throwing himself onto the tracks in front of a train. Suffering from an illness with symptoms similar to tuberculosis that doctors were unable to diagnose, he spent most of the years 1917 and 1918 in hospitals and sanatoria in Wells, Matlock, and London.

During a visit to one of Ramanujan's hospital rooms, Hardy remarked that the taxicab in which he had just ridden had a boring number, 1729. Ramanujan quickly replied that it was actually an interesting number because it was the smallest number that could be written as the sum of two cubes in two different ways—as $12^3 + 1^3 = 1728 + 1 = 1729$ and as $10^3 + 9^3 = 1000 + 729 = 1729$—a discovery that he had made and had recorded in his notebooks while in India. After Hardy shared the story, now known as the taxicab problem, mathematicians started investigating Ramanujan's claim and other numbers with related mathematical properties. Today a set of four integers a, b, c, and d that satisfy the equation $a^3 + b^3 = c^3 + d^3$ are called Ramanujan numbers. Mathematicians have proven that there are infinitely many such sets of numbers.

Return to India, 1919–1920

In February 1919, after the war ended and his health improved, Ramanujan sailed to India, where he arrived as a celebrated and accomplished mathematician. The University of Madras offered him a five-year appointment as a research mathematician with an annual stipend of £250. Trinity College promised to fund his travel expenses, enabling him to continue his research partnership with Hardy. Despite his continuing health problems, he worked ambitiously, investigating new ideas in mathematics. In January 1920 he wrote to Hardy that he had discovered a concept that he called "mock theta functions," infinite sums of rational expressions such as

$$\phi(q) = 1 + \frac{q}{\left(1+q^2\right)} + \frac{q^4}{\left(1+q^2\right)\cdot\left(1+q^4\right)} + \frac{q^7}{\left(1+q^2\right)\cdot\left(1+q^4\right)\cdot\left(1+q^6\right)} + \cdots.$$

He recorded 650 results about mock theta functions on 130 sheets of loose paper that mathematicians came to call his "Lost Notebook" because after his death they remained hidden in a library in Madras until 1976.

Ramanujan worked on his mathematical research until four days before he died. When he became so involved in his work that he refused to stop for meals, his wife, Janaki, would feed him rice while he continued to work. On April 26, 1920, 32-year-old Ramanujan died of hepatic amoebiasis, a parasitic infection of the liver and intestines, at a rented home in Chetput near Madras.

Fifteen years after Ramanujan's death, Hardy offered his personal rankings of mathematicians on the basis of pure talent. On a scale from one to 100, he rated himself a 25 and Ramanujan a 100. In the years since his death, the 4,000 theorems that Ramanujan wrote in his notebooks have been studied extensively by mathematicians from around the world. They have determined that about two-thirds of these results were not known to other mathematicians at the time that he discovered them. In 2005 the Abdus Salam International Centre for Theoretical Physics and the International Mathematical Union honored his memory by establishing the Ramanujan Prize to be awarded annually to a young mathematician from a developing country.

Conclusion

Despite his lack of formal training in higher mathematics, Ramanujan was a creative mathematician whose insight into algebraic formulas and infinite series enabled him to make significant contributions to number theory. He created new techniques for approximating π that mathematicians continue to employ and introduced the analysis of highly composite numbers. The methods he developed to determine the number of prime factors of a positive integer led to the establishment of probabilistic number theory. His asymptotic formula for the number of partitions of a positive integer introduced the circle method, which led to significant developments in additive number theory. Mathematicians continue to study the mock theta functions he discovered as well as the thousands of formulas from his notebooks.

FURTHER READING

Berndt, Bruce C., and Robert A. Rankin. *Ramanujan: Letters and Commentary*. Providence, R.I.: American Mathematical Society, 1995. Photographs and letters about mathematics and other topics from all periods of Ramanujan's life.

——, eds. *Ramanujan: Essays and Surveys*. Providence, R.I.: American Mathematical Society, 2001. Collection of essays written by various mathematicians about Ramanujan's life and his mathematical work.

Hardy, G. H. *Ramanujan: Twelve Lectures on Subjects Suggested by His Life and Work*. New York: Chelsea Publishing, 1940. Hardy's lectures about Ramanujan provide an overview of his life and work.

Hardy, G. H., P. V. Seshu Aiyar, and B. M. Wilson. *Collected Papers of Srinivasa Ramanujan*. New York: Chelsea Publishing, 1962. Complete collection of Ramanujan's 37 mathematical research papers, with a biographical sketch by Hardy.

Henderson, Harry. "Srinivasa Ramanujan (1887–1920)." In *Modern Mathematicians*, 58–69. New York: Facts On File, 1996. Biographical sketch with a discussion of his mathematics.

James, Ioan. "Srinivasa Iyengar Ramanujan." In *Remarkable Mathematicians from Euler to von Neumann*, 357–362. Washington, D.C.: Mathematical Association of America, 2003. Brief biography and description of his mathematics.

Kanigel, Robert. *The Man Who Knew Infinity. A Life of the Genius Ramanujan*. New York: Scribner, 1991. Detailed biography.

O'Connor, J. J., and E. F. Robertson. "Srinivasa Aiyangar Ramanujan." MacTutor History of Mathematics Archive, University of Saint Andrews. Available online. URL: http://www-groups.dcs.st-andrews.ac.uk/~history/Mathematicians/Ramanujan.html. Accessed December 29, 2003. Biography from the University of Saint Andrews, Scotland.

Ore, Øystein. "Ramanujan, Srinivasa Aiyangar." In *Dictionary of Scientific Biography*, Vol. 5, edited by Charles C. Gillispie, 267–269. New York: Scribner, 1972. Encyclopedic biography, including a detailed description of his mathematical writings.

Reimer, Luetta, and Wilbert Reimer. "Numbers Were His Greatest Treasure: Srinivasa Ramanujan." In *Mathematicians Are People, Too: Stories from the Lives of Great Mathematicians,* 122–132. Parsippany, N.J.: Seymour, 1990. Life story with historical facts and fictionalized dialogue; intended for elementary school students.

Sankaran, Neeraja. "S. I. Ramanujan, 1887–1920, Indian Number Theorist." In *Notable Mathematicians: From Ancient Times to the Present,* edited by Robyn V. Young, 411–413. Detroit, Mich.: Gale, 1998. Brief but informative profile of Ramanujan and his work.

6

Norbert Wiener

(1894–1964)

Norbert Wiener provided a mathematical explanation for Brownian motion, established a rigorous mathematical basis for classical potential theory, and founded the discipline of cybernetics. *(Massachusetts Institute of Technology Museum and Historical Collections, courtesy of AIP Emilio Segrè Visual Archives)*

Father of Cybernetics

Norbert Wiener (pronounced WEE-ner) was a child prodigy who discovered new mathematical techniques to solve a range of applied problems in pure mathematics, physics, biology, and engineering. His introduction of the Wiener measure provided a mathematical explanation for Brownian motion and led to advances in probability and stochastic processes. The Wiener criterion and his analysis of the Dirichlet problem established a rigorous mathematical basis for classical potential theory. His work in general harmonic analysis and Tauberian theorems provided techniques for the investigation of nonperiodic phenomena. He founded the discipline of cybernetics, to which he introduced statistical methods to understand and manage interactions between humans and machines.

Child Prodigy

Norbert Wiener was born on November 26, 1894, in Columbia, Missouri, to Leo Wiener, a professor of modern languages at the University of Missouri, and Bertha Kahn, the daughter of a department store owner. In 1895 his father accepted a position as a professor of Slavic languages and literature at Harvard University and moved the family to Massachusetts. As a young child, Wiener showed signs of brilliance, learning to read when he was three years old. Tutored at home by his father and encouraged to read in his father's extensive library, he became a child prodigy, entering high school at the age of nine. He graduated from Ayer High School when he was 11 and earned his bachelor's degree in mathematics from Tufts College in Medford, Massachusetts at the age of 14. After studying a year of zoology at Harvard University and then a year of philosophy at Cornell University, he returned to Harvard to complete a Ph.D. in philosophy by 1913, at the age of 18. His dissertation in mathematical logic, titled "A Comparison of the Algebra of Relatives of Schroeder and of Whitehead and Russell," compared the system of logic developed by Welsh mathematician Bertrand Russell and English mathematician Alfred North Whitehead in their *Principia mathematica* (Principles of mathematics) with the earlier algebraic system created by German mathematician Ernst Schroeder.

Supported by a one-year fellowship from Harvard University, he traveled to Europe, where he wrote papers on philosophy and worked with several leading international mathematicians. At England's Cambridge University he studied the philosophy of mathematics with Russell and complex variables and Lebesgue integration under the direction of Godfrey Hardy. In 1914 he traveled to the University of Göttingen, in Germany, where he studied differential equations with David Hilbert and group theory with Edmund Landau. While in England he wrote and published his first paper, a brief treatise on set theory titled "On a Method of Rearranging the Positive Integers in a Series of Ordinal Numbers Greater Than That of Any Given Fundamental Sequence of Omegas," which appeared in 1913 in the journal *Messenger of Mathematics*. In 1914 his paper titled "The Highest Good" won a Bowdoin Prize for philosophical essays written by Harvard students or graduates and was published in the *Journal of Philosophy, Psychology, and Scientific Methods*. Among the 15 papers he published on philosophy and logic before focusing his attention on mathematics, Wiener considered the most significant one to be his 1914 paper "A Simplification of the Logic of Relations" that appeared in the *Proceedings of the Cambridge Philosophical Society*. In it he described a method for reducing the theory of relations to the theory of classes.

Shortly before the outbreak of World War I, in June 1914, Wiener returned to the United States, where he held a variety of temporary positions during the next five years. He lectured on mathematical logic at Harvard University during the academic year 1915–16 and was an instructor of mathematics at the University of Maine for the following academic year. After graduating from Reserve Officer Training School at Harvard, he worked briefly in the engineer training program at General Electric Company in Lynn, Massachusetts, running steam consumption tests on turbine engines, and spent a year as a staff writer for *Encyclopedia Americana* in Albany, New York. In 1918, at the invitation of mathematician Oswald Veblin, he joined the ballistics group at the Aberdeen Proving Ground in Maryland. There he participated with other mathematicians in the calculation of range tables for new army artillery and ammunition based on the gun's angle of elevation, the size of the charges, wind speed, air pressure, and other variable factors. After the end of the war, he worked as a reporter for the *Boston Herald* newspaper, writing stories on the presidential candidacy of General Clarence Edwards and the plight of immigrant laborers in the textile mills of Lawrence, Massachusetts.

In 1919 Wiener secured a position as an instructor of mathematics at the Massachusetts Institute of Technology (MIT). At the time of his appointment, the mathematics department was primarily a service department that taught courses to prepare students for careers in science and engineering. His initial responsibilities were to teach calculus classes to undergraduates 20 hours per week. During his 41 years on the faculty, Wiener helped transform the mathematics department by engaging in an ambitious program of research, developing research collaborations with other departments at the university, and attracting a large number of capable mathematicians. His productive work helped establish MIT's reputation as one of the country's leading schools for research in both pure and applied mathematics.

Harmonic Analysis

Wiener's first major research project at MIT involved the mathematical analysis of Brownian motion. In 1827 British botanist Robert Brown had observed and studied the rapid movements of pollen and other organic particles suspended in water. While studying the phenomenon in 1905, German physicist Albert Einstein had theorized that water molecules randomly collided with the floating particles, causing them to move erratically. By studying the collection of paths of individual particles, Wiener showed that almost all paths were continuous but nondifferentiable due to their sudden changes in direction. In his 1921 paper "The Average of an Analytical Functional and the Brownian Movement," which appeared in the *Proceedings of the National Academy of Sciences*, he introduced a technique known as the Wiener measure that produced an average for the collection of paths by assigning probabilities to the individual paths. He presented a more generalized formulation of this method in a 1923 paper, "Differential Space," that appeared in MIT's *Journal of Mathematics and Physics*. This highly theoretical work remained relatively unnoticed for two decades until Paul Lévy in France and Andrei Kolmogorov in Russia used it as the basis for the theory of stochastic processes and the modern theory of probability. The Wiener measure allows researchers to construct mathematical models to study the net effect of a large number of tiny contributions from mutually independent sources in applications such as stock market averages and the transmission of distorted electrical signals.

Changing the focus of his research, Wiener investigated a fundamental problem in electrostatics: the determination of the shapes that permitted electrical conductors to carry a fixed charge without spontaneously discharging. His research on this question led him to the more general Dirichlet problem, the determination of functions that have well-behaved derivatives in a given region and that take specified values on its boundary. In his 1923 paper "Nets and the Dirichlet Problem" written with MIT mathematics colleague Henry Bayard Phillips and published in the *Journal of Mathematics and Physics*, he presented some initial results about electric fields determined by a rectangular arrangement of conductors. His 1924 paper "The Dirichlet Problem," which also appeared in the *Journal of Mathematics and Physics*, resolved many questions about spontaneous discharge, presented a fuller treatment of the Dirichlet problem, and had a major impact on potential theory, the study of electric, magnetic, and gravitational fields. Another 1924 paper, "Une condition nécessaire et suffisante de possibilité pour le problème de Dirichlet" (A necessary and sufficient condition of possibility for the Dirichlet problem), that appeared in *Comptes rendus de l'Académie des Sciences de Paris* (Rendering of the accounts the Academy of Sciences of Paris) introduced a test now known as the Wiener criterion to determine the points on a conductor at which the voltage was discontinuous. In this group of papers he addressed the specific question in electrostatics by describing all shapes for which unstable charges occurred and provided a larger framework for more general questions by establishing a rigorous mathematical basis for classical potential theory.

Throughout the decade of the 1920s, Wiener experienced changes in his personal and professional life, as well as finding additional opportunities for collaborative research. In 1924 MIT promoted him to the rank of assistant professor. Two years later he married Margaret Engemann, an assistant professor of modern languages at Juniata College in Pennsylvania. Supported by a Guggenheim fellowship for the academic year 1926–27, Wiener and his wife visited England, Germany, Switzerland, Italy, and Denmark.

During their travels he conducted research with mathematicians whom he had met on his previous trips to Europe, established working relationships with new colleagues, and developed ideas for generalizing the work he had already published. A year after the Wieners returned to the United States, their first child, Barbara, was born. In 1929 they had another daughter, Peggy, and MIT promoted Wiener to the rank of associate professor.

Wiener's research in the late 1920s focused on mathematical techniques for processing electrical signals. Mathematicians and engineers used the technique of Fourier analysis to decompose a periodic signal that repeated a regular pattern into an infinite sum of sine waves. In his 1930 paper "Generalized Harmonic Analysis," which appeared in the journal *Acta Mathematica* (Mathematical activities), he developed a more general technique that extended this analysis to nonperiodic signals. In this paper he introduced the technique of autocorrelation to measure the average energy in a signal over intervals of time. Proving equations such as

$$\lim_{\mu \to 0} \frac{1}{2\mu} \int_{-\infty}^{\infty} |s(u+\mu) - s(u-\mu)|^2 \, du = \lim_{T \to \infty} \frac{1}{2T} \int_{-T}^{T} |f(x)|^2 \, dx, \quad \text{he devel-}$$

oped a general theory for showing the equivalence of different weighted averages of measurable functions and spectral distributions.

This work with generalized harmonic analysis led Wiener to develop numerous Tauberian theorems, results about the weighted averages of divergent infinite series. His 1932 paper "Tauberian Theorems," published in the *Annals of Mathematics*, won the 1933 Bôcher Memorial Prize from the American Mathematical Society (AMS) for the quality of work and originality of exposition. Among the many results presented in this 100-page paper was an elegant proof of the prime number theorem, the important principle of number theory stating that the probability of an integer N being prime is approximately $\dfrac{1}{\ln(N)}$. His innovative work with gener-

alized harmonic analysis and its consequences for infinite series established Wiener's reputation as an accomplished mathematician. In 1932 MIT promoted him to the rank of full professor, and in 1933 the National Academy of Sciences elected him as a fellow.

This international reputation enabled Wiener to collaborate for extended periods of time with mathematicians at foreign institutions and to bring distinguished colleagues to MIT as visiting scholars. Through these collaborative efforts, in the early 1930s he contributed new results to Fourier analysis, the branch of mathematics concerned with expressing a function as an infinite sum of sine and cosine waves. He brought Austrian mathematician Eberhard Hopf to MIT to work on the solutions to integral equations that arose in ergodic theory where the average value of a function played a central role. Their joint paper "Über eine Klasse singulärer Integralgleichungen" (On a singular class of integral equations), which appeared in 1931 in *Sitzungsberichte Deutsch Akademie Wissenschaften zu Berlin, Klasse Mathematisch-Physikalische-Technische* (Conference proceedings of the German Academy of Sciences at Berlin, mathematical-physical-technological class),

introduced the Wiener-Hopf equation $f(x) = \int_0^\infty K(x-y)f(y)dy$

that became important in Wiener's later research in the 1940s and 1950s. He spent the academic year 1931–32 at Cambridge University delivering a series of lectures on his recent work in Fourier analysis. In 1933 he published these lectures as the book *The Fourier Integral and Certain of Its Applications*. When he returned to MIT the following year, he brought with him Raymond Paley, a young English mathematician from Cambridge University. The two researchers coauthored the 1934 book *Fourier Transforms in the Complex Domain*, which presented new results about complex-valued functions.

In the late 1930s Wiener broadened the collection of applications that he successfully analyzed using techniques of integration by addressing chaos and ergodic theory. In his 1938 paper "The Homogeneous Chaos," published in the *American Journal of Mathematics*, he generalized the mathematical explanation of random motion that he had developed to describe Brownian motion and applied his broader techniques to other situations involving the nonlinear, random movement of particles such as air turbulence, fluid flows, and noise in the transmission of an electrical signal. His 1939 paper "The Ergodic Theorem," which appeared in the *Duke Mathematical Journal*, reproved and extended the ergodic theorem about the random but well-behaved motion of particles. In the following decades physicists built on his ideas to develop theories in quantum mechanics.

Research during the War Years

As World War II approached, in the late 1930s Wiener became involved with several programs to aid in the war effort. He worked with the Emergency Committee in Aid of Displaced Foreign Scholars to secure housing accommodations and visiting appointments at U.S. universities for European mathematicians and scientists who were fleeing their homelands. In 1940 he joined the War Preparedness Committee that had been jointly established by the AMS and the Mathematical Association of America to organize mathematicians to work on applications with potential military uses.

Working for the government's Office of Scientific Research and Development (OSRD), Wiener sketched out the preliminary design of a computer capable of mechanically solving differential equations. Rather than modify existing calculating machines that represented numbers in decimal notation as sums of powers of 10, he envisioned a binary, or base-two, machine that would represent numerical values as sums of powers of two, a notation in which

1101.101 would indicate $2^3 + 2^2 + 2^0 + 2^{-1} + 2^{-3} = 8 + 4 + 1 + \dfrac{1}{2} + \dfrac{1}{8} =$

13.625. He planned to store data on magnetic tapes and to employ a Monte Carlo method to solve differential equations by averaging the results determined by large sets of random data. Although his supervisor rejected his preliminary report, Wiener's visionary ideas of binary representation, magnetic tape storage, and Monte Carlo algorithms became standard features of multipurpose digital computers in subsequent decades.

Later in 1940 Wiener secured a grant from OSRD to develop a more effective fire-control apparatus for anti-aircraft guns. As part of their solution of the problem, his research team developed two algorithms that were extensions of his previous work on the Wiener-Hopf equation. They devised a filtering technique to minimize the error in the radar signal used to track the path of a targeted aircraft by separating the actual message from the distorting noise. They also created an extrapolation algorithm to statistically predict where a targeted plane would likely fly in the next 20 seconds based on its path in the previous 10 seconds. Wiener's most innovative contribution to the solution of the problem was to treat the human operator of a gun as a component in the tracking and firing process. His team developed a hybrid control process that combined input from the operator with the results of the mechanized filtering and extrapolation algorithms.

Wiener amplified his ideas on negative feedback loops and human-machine interaction in a 1942 classified report titled *Extrapolation, Interpolation and Smoothing of Stationary Time Series with Engineering Applications.* Nicknamed the "Yellow Peril" for the color of its cover and the difficulty of the subject matter, this handbook was widely used during the later stages of the war by designers of systems to control the aiming and firing of antiaircraft guns. In 1949 he produced an amplified version of the book that addressed industrial applications and influenced the design of automated control systems and electrical communication equipment. The statistical treatment of prediction theory and communication theory described in this book led to a general statistical point of view in communication engineering that has been gradually adopted in meteorology, sociology, and economics.

At the end of the war Wiener publicly voiced his strong opinions on social issues. After the U.S. government decided to drop atomic bombs on two Japanese cities in 1945, he became a vocal opponent of military conflict and declined to participate in conferences and research projects that had potential military applications. He expressed his opposition to war and to the development of weapons of destruction in two letters: "A Scientist Rebels," which appeared in 1947 in the *Atlantic Monthly* magazine, and "A Rebellious Scientist after Two Years," which was published in 1948 in the *Bulletin of Atomic Scientists.* He cautioned his mathematical and scientific colleagues to consider the moral implications of their research and its impact on society. He also considered the consequences of computer-controlled machinery and the advent of automatic factories in which human workers would be regimented or eliminated. In a 1949 presentation to the Society for the Advancement of Management and a 1952 talk to the American Society of Mechanical Engineers, he discussed the advantages and risks of automation and encouraged the members of these groups to ensure that displaced workers became trained for thoughtful work as troubleshooters, skilled craftsworkers, and programming special-ists. His 1950 book, *The Human Use of Human Beings*, stressed the social implications of embracing a highly mechanized society.

Cybernetics

The interaction between humans and machines and the analysis of the human body as a machine became the focus of Wiener's research from the mid-1940s to the end of his career 20 years later. With Mexican physiologist Arturo Rosenblueth, he used a statistical theory of time series analysis to model the electrical signals carried in human brain waves. Using MIT's autocorrelation machine and collaborating with researchers at Massachusetts General Hospital, Wiener and Rosenblueth determined that the flow of electrical impulses from nerve to nerve was similar to the discrete process of electrical current in computer circuits. They explained their work in many articles, including the 1946 paper "The Mathematical Formulation of the Problem of Conduction of Impulses in a Network of Connected Excitable Elements, Specifically in Cardiac Muscle" that appeared in *Archivos del Instituto de Cardiología de México* (Archives of the Mexican Institute of Cardiology).

Wiener concentrated his research on the methods used by the human machine to communicate and to control its own function-ing. He worked to develop an interactive iron lung that would allow signals from patients' nervous systems to influence the operation of the artificial breathing device as their muscles learned to breathe again. His 1949 paper "Sound Communication with the Deaf," published in the journal *Philosophy of Science*, explored possible ways to convey sound impulses to the hearing impaired through patterns of pressure applied to the skin. In his 1951 paper "Problems of Sensory Prosthesis," which appeared in the *Bulletin of the American Mathematical Society*, he discussed methods that would allow patients to manipulate mentally artificial limbs. He investigated homeostatic processes such as blood pressure, body temperature, and balance in which the human body maintains a measure of equilibrium through semiautomatic systems of negative feedback that enable it to react to deviations from the norm. He published his findings on this subject in a 1951 paper, "Homeostasis in the Individual and Society," that appeared in the *Journal of the Franklin Institute* and a 1953 paper, "The Concept of Homeostasis in Medicine," that appeared in the *Transactions and Studies of the College of Physicians of Philadelphia.*

These individual projects were part of Wiener's larger research program on systems of control, communications, and organization. He introduced the word *cybernetics*, from the Greek word *kubernētēs*, meaning "steersman," to describe this new field of study. His approach involved creating a mathematical framework to express the interdependence between various components in a structure, system, or organization. He contended that since most systems functioned on partial or imprecise information, statistical methods had to play central roles in the interplay between information theory, prediction theory, and communication theory. Despite its heavily mathematical explanations, his 1948 book, *Cybernetics, or Control and Communication in the Animal and the Machine*, became a bestseller and introduced the terms *feedback, stability, homeostasis, prediction*, and *filtering* into common usage. The prevalence of nonlinear methods in the mathematical foundation of cybernetics led Wiener to write his 1958 book, *Nonlinear Problems in Random Theory.* These books and his significant contributions to the establishment of the field earned Wiener the title "Father of Cybernetics."

Wiener's work in cybernetics generated interest and recognition throughout the international scientific community. In 1949 the AMS selected him to deliver a talk on prostheses for the prestigious Joshua Gibbs lecture at their annual meeting. As a Fulbright fellow in 1950–51, he lectured about cybernetics in Britain, Spain, France,

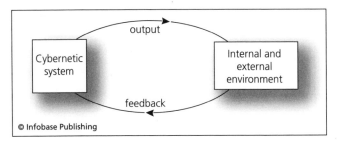

A cybernetic system uses information about changes in its internal or external environment to adjust its output in order to amplify (positive feedback) or counteract (negative feedback) these changes.

and Mexico. In subsequent years he traveled to India, Japan, and China, sharing with scientists and mathematicians his work on mathematical explanations of the functioning of the human body and on his analysis of human-machine interaction.

In his later years Wiener wrote an increasing number of works for nontechnical audiences. He wrote two short stories, titled "The Brain" and "Miracle of the Broom Closet," that appeared in two 1952 issues of *Technology and Engineering News*. In his two-part autobiography, *Ex-Prodigy. My Childhood and Youth*, published in 1953, and *I Am a Mathematician. The Later Life of a Prodigy*, which appeared three years later, he reflected on his life as a mathematician and his relationships with his professional colleagues. After he retired from MIT in 1959, he wrote a novel titled *The Tempter* about an idealistic scientist and tried to interest film director Orson Welles in developing the story into a movie. He continued to expound on moral and social themes, publishing the 1960 paper "Some Moral and Technical Consequences of Automation" in *Science* and the 1964 book *God and Golem, Inc.: A Comment on Certain Points Where Cybernetics Impinges on Religion*. He died in Stockholm, Sweden, after suffering a heart attack, on March 18, 1964, two months after President Lyndon Johnson had awarded him the National Medal of Science.

After Wiener's death several organizations made efforts to honor his lifetime of work. The AMS paid tribute to him by printing a special issue of their *Bulletin* in 1966 that described his contributions to eight areas of mathematics and science. In 1967 the mathematics department at MIT, the AMS, and the Society for Industrial and Applied Mathematics established the Norbert Wiener Prize in Applied Mathematics, a $5,000 prize awarded every three years for an outstanding contribution to the field of applied mathematics. The Computer Professionals for Social Responsibility instituted the annual Norbert Wiener Award for Social and Professional Responsibility in 1987 to recognize computer professionals for socially responsible uses of computers.

Conclusion

In his lengthy professional career Norbert Wiener published more than 200 books and papers that developed applications of mathematics to problems that could be stated in physical terms. His research on Brownian motion and his development of the Wiener measure led to advances in probability and stochastic processes. In the area of harmonic analysis and Tauberian theorems, he developed techniques to investigate nonperiodic phenomena. His work with control systems for antiaircraft guns, human brain waves, and human-machine interaction led to the founding of cybernetics.

FURTHER READING

Drucker, Thomas. "Norbert Wiener, 1894–1964, American Logician." In *Notable Mathematicians: From Ancient Times to the Present,* edited by Robyn V. Young, 512–515. Detroit, Mich.: Gale, 1998. Brief but informative profile of Wiener and his work.

Freudenthal, Hans. "Wiener, Norbert." In *Dictionary of Scientific Biography,* Vol. 14, edited by Charles C. Gillispie, 344–347. New York: Scribner, 1972. Encyclopedic biography, including a detailed description of his mathematical writings.

Heims, Steve J. *John Von Neumann and Norbert Wiener: From Mathematics to the Technologies of Life and Death.* Cambridge, Mass.: MIT Press, 1980. Historical work documenting the contributions of these two mathematicians to the development of computers with military applications.

James, Ioan. "Norbert Wiener." In *Remarkable Mathematicians from Euler to von Neumann,* 386–392. Washington, D.C.: Mathematical Association of America, 2003. Brief biography and description of his mathematics.

Jerison, David, and Daniel Stroock. "Norbert Wiener." *Notices of the American Mathematical Society* 42, no. 4 (1995): 430–438. Article in a mathematics journal providing a biographical sketch of Wiener.

Mandrekar, V. "Mathematical Work of Norbert Wiener." *Notices of the American Mathematical Society* 42, no. 4 (1995): 664–669. Article in a mathematics journal providing a detailed description of his work.

Masani, Pesi R. *Norbert Wiener, 1894–1964.* Boston: Birkhäuser, 1990. Detailed biography with extensive appendices.

O'Connor, J. J., and E. F. Robertson. "Norbert Wiener." MacTutor History of Mathematics Archive, University of Saint Andrews. Available online. URL: http://www-groups.dcs.st-andrews. ac.uk/~history/Mathematicians/Wiener_Norbert.html. Accessed March 18, 2003. Biography from the University of Saint Andrews, Scotland.

Wiener, Norbert. *Cybernetics, or Control and Communication in the Animal and the Machine.* Cambridge, Mass.: MIT Press, 1961. The classic work by the father of cybernetics.

———. *Ex-Prodigy. My Childhood and Youth.* Cambridge, Mass.: MIT Press, 1953. The first part of Wiener's autobiography.

———. *I Am a Mathematician. The Later Life of a Prodigy. An Autobiographical Account of the Mature Years and Career of Norbert Wiener and a Continuation of the Account of His Childhood in Ex-Prodigy.* Garden City, N.Y.: Doubleday, 1956. The second part of Wiener's autobiography.

John von Neumann

(1903–1957)

John von Neumann developed the theory of von Neumann algebras, established game theory as a rigorous branch of mathematics, popularized the von Neumann architecture for computers, and helped to develop nuclear weapons. *(The Granger Collection)*

Mathematics for Science and Technology

After establishing his reputation as an accomplished pure mathematician, John von Neumann (pronounced von NOY-man) made significant contributions to several branches of science and technology. Early in his career he introduced a new definition of ordinal numbers in set theory, developed the theory of von Neumann algebras, established game theory as a rigorous branch of mathematics, and introduced a new axiomatic basis for quantum mechanics. In the latter half of his career he developed the von Neumann architecture for computers, applied the concepts of game theory to economics, introduced new computer algorithms for numerical analysis, helped to develop nuclear weapons, and used cellular automata to model the reproduction of biological organisms.

Early Research in Set Theory

János Lajos Neumann was born on December 28, 1903, in Budapest, Hungary. He was the oldest of three sons of Max Neumann, a prosperous banker, and Margit Kann, the daughter of a prominent businessman. In 1913 his father purchased a title of nobility and formally changed the family name to Neumann von Margitta. János, who was nicknamed Jancsi as a child, later anglicized his name to John von Neumann. As a child he learned to speak Hungarian, English, German, and French and to read Latin and Greek. At the age of six he could divide eight-digit numbers in his head. He entertained family visitors by reciting names, addresses, and phone numbers that he had memorized from the telephone directory.

Von Neumann was educated at home by tutors until the age of 10, when he entered Lutheran Gymnasium, a private elementary and secondary school in Budapest. Recognizing that he had already mastered most of the standard mathematics curriculum, the school's administrators arranged for him to be tutored by professors from the University of Budapest. At the age of 17 he coauthored an original research paper with Michael Fekete, one of his tutors from the university. The article, titled "Über die Lage der Nullstellen gewisser Minimumpolynome" (On the location of the zero sets of certain minimum polynomials) and published in 1922 in *Jahresbericht der Deutsche Mathematiker-Vereinigung* (Annual report of the Association of German Mathematicians) generalized a theorem about the roots of a particular class of polynomial functions.

When von Neumann completed his studies at the gymnasium in 1921, he enrolled as a mathematics student at the University of Budapest and as a chemistry major at the University of Berlin in Germany. He attended classes in Berlin, traveling to Budapest only at the end of each semester to take his final examinations. In 1923 the Hungarian journal *Acta Universitatis Szegediensis*

(Activities at the University of Szeged) published his paper "Zur Einfuhrung der transfiniten Ordnungszahlen" (On the introduction of the transfinite ordinal numbers) in which he gave a definition of ordinal numbers that improved on the original formulation of the concept, introduced 50 years earlier by Russian mathematician Georg Cantor. After two years of study in Berlin, he transferred to Eidgenössische Technische Hochschule (Federal Institute of Technology) in Zurich, Switzerland, where he earned his diploma in chemical engineering in 1925. He received a Ph.D. in mathematics from the University of Budapest the following year, submitting a doctoral dissertation titled "Az áltálanos Halmazelmélet axiomatikus felépitése" (An axiomatic construction of universal set theory) in which he proposed a new set of axioms for set theory.

Von Neumann received a Rockefeller Fellowship for the academic year 1926–27, enabling him to continue his research in set theory with German mathematician David Hilbert at the University of Göttingen in Germany. He lectured in mathematics as a *Privatdozent* (assistant professor) at the University of Berlin from 1926 to 1929 and at the University of Hamburg the following year. He participated in Hilbert's program to prove that mathematical theory was free from contradiction and to establish a rigorous axiomatic foundation from which all mathematical results could be proven. In his 1927 paper "Zur Hilbertschen Beweistheorie" (On the Hilbert theory of proof) that appeared in *Mathematische Zeitschrift* (Mathematical reviews), he showed that the collection of mathematical results that could be obtained using finitely many logical steps formed a consistent subsystem of mathematics. His 1928 paper "Die Axiomatisierung der Mengenlehre" (The axiomatization of set theory), which was also published in *Mathematische Zeitschrift*, expanded on his doctoral dissertation. In this work he presented a concise list of axioms and demonstrated how most of set theory could be derived from them. In 1931 Austro-Hungarian logician Kurt Gödel rendered the goals of the Hilbert program impossible when he proved the incompleteness theorem, the principle that every axiomatic mathematical system included propositions that could neither be proved nor disproved. Before leaving the discipline of set theory, von Neumann proved additional theorems about decompositions of intervals of real numbers, solvable groups, Haar measure, and linear topological spaces.

Quantum Theory

Von Neumann extended his work with axiomatic systems, making fundamental contributions to the new discipline of quantum theory, the branch of mathematical physics concerned with the study of subatomic particles. In a series of papers that he wrote between 1927 and 1929, he developed the mathematical framework of quantum mechanics by applying the techniques of Hermitian operators on infinite dimensional Hilbert spaces. Within this mathematical structure he presented a finite set of axioms that unified both the wave and particle theories of quantum mechanics. His influential papers on the subject included the 1927 paper "Über die Grundlagen der Quantenmechanik" (On the foundations of quantum mechanics), published in *Mathematische Annalen* (Annals of mathematics), that he coauthored with Hilbert and German physicist Lothar Nordheim; a pair of 1928 papers written with Hungarian physicist Eugene Wigner titled "Zur Erklärung einiger Eigenschaften der Spektren aus der Quantenmechanik des Drehelektrons, I, II" (On a united explanation of the spectral properties for the quantum mechanics of rotating electrons, I, II), which appeared in *Zeitschrift fur Physik* (Reviews of physics); and a 1929 paper from *Mathematische Annalen* titled "Allgemeine Eigenwerttheorie Hermitescher Funcktionaloperatoren" (General theory of eigenvalues for Hermitian functional operators).

In his 1932 book *Mathematische Grundlagen der Quantenmechanik* (*Mathematical Foundations of Quantum Mechanics*), von Neumann presented a comprehensive summary of his axiomatic formulation of quantum physics. He devoted two chapters of the book to an analysis of the question of causality versus indeterminacy, concluding that the introduction of hidden parameters in an attempt to explain completely events was inconsistent with the basic structure of quantum theory. The work made contributions to the theory of quantum measurement by discussing how the process of observation interfered with the measurement of the phenomenon being studied. The book also included a discussion of the weak ergodic theorem about the statistical distribution of particles that he had proven earlier in the year in his paper "Proof of the Quasi-Ergodic Hypothesis," published in the *Proceedings of the National Academy of Sciences*.

By the time his book on quantum mechanics appeared, von Neumann enjoyed an international reputation as a mathematician and had relocated to America. In 1929 he married Marietta Koevesi, an economics student at the University of Budapest. The following year they moved to the United States, where he accepted an appointment as a visiting professor at Princeton University, in New Jersey. He remained at the university until 1933, when he joined the newly founded Institute for Advanced Studies in Princeton as one of the six original mathematics professors, along with James Alexander, Albert Einstein, Marston Morse, Oswald Veblen, and Hermann Weyl. In 1933 he also became coeditor of the journals *Annals of Mathematics* and *Compositio Mathematica* (Compilation of mathematics). His only child, Marina, was born in 1936. After divorcing his first wife in 1937, he traveled to Poland to marry his second wife, Klára Dán, who later became one of the first computer programmers.

Game Theory

One of von Neumann's research areas in the 1930s was game theory, the mathematical study of competition and cooperation. In the 1920s he had studied two-person zero-sum games in which two competing participants made choices that resulted in a payoff for one player and a penalty of equal magnitude for the other. In his 1928 article "Zur Theorie der Gesellschaftsspiele" (On the theory of games of strategy), published in *Mathematische Annalen*, he had proven the minimax principle that in any two-person zero-sum game, each player had one optimal strategy. This paper also provided a formal definition of a game among n players, formalizing ideas that had been introduced in 1921 by French mathematician Émile Borel and establishing a rigorous mathematical basis for game theory.

In his 1937 paper "Über ein ökonomisches Gleichungssystem und eine Verallgemeinerung des Brouwerschen Fixpunktsatzes" (On a model of general economic equilibrium and an application of the Brouwer fixed point theorem), which appeared in the Austrian monograph *Ergebnisse eines mathematischen Kolloquium 1935–36* (Outcome of a mathematical colloquium, 1935–36), he applied the theoretical concepts of game theory to the discipline of economics. This influential paper introduced a variety of quantitative techniques to explain mathematically economic phenomena, including price-cost and demand-supply inequalities, activity analysis production sets, steady-state growth, saddlepoint characterizations, and complementary slackness conditions. Using the Brouwer fixed point theorem from topology and other results from geometry, von Neumann proved that good strategies existed under very general conditions. With mathematical models he showed that the rate of interest is related to the rate of growth rather than the quantity of capital in an economy. Economists use the term the *von Neumann revolution* to describe the collection of changes this paper brought to the economic study of equilibrium, growth, and capital.

In 1944 von Neumann coauthored the *Theory of Games and Economic Behavior* with German economist Oskar Morgenstern. This book provided an axiomatic basis for the theories of utility and choice under uncertainty that modeled the behavior of an economic player who must select a strategy with only probabilistic knowledge of the value of the available options. Von Neumann and Morgenstern broadly applied the concepts of game theory to situations involving coalitions in which economic players cooperate with one another, monopolies in which there is no competition, and free trade among multiple participants. This seminal work in mathematical economics significantly influenced the international practice of economic theory.

Von Neumann maintained his interest in this branch of mathematics, continuing to write on various topics within game theory throughout his career. In 1953 he coauthored two chapters for the book *Contributions to Theory of Games, Volume I*. In "Solutions of Games by Differential Equations," he and American mathematician George W. Brown used the continuous techniques of analysis to solve game theory problems that were stated discretely. The chapter "Two Variants of Poker" that he wrote with his doctoral students Donald B. Gillies and John P. Mayberry demonstrated the applicability of game theory to a situation that combined both chance and strategy. His 1954 paper "A Numerical Method to Determine Optimum Strategy," which appeared in *Naval Research Logistics Quarterly*, presented computer-based solutions that he had helped to develop and implement for military applications.

Operator Theory

Nearly one-third of von Neumann's published works dealt with the branch of algebra known as operator theory. In his research on quantum mechanics he had introduced new ideas in the study of infinite dimensional Hilbert spaces that led to the reformulation of the theory of bounded and unbounded symmetric operators. His 1929 article "Zur Theorie der unbeschränkten Matrizen" (On the theory of unbounded matrices), published in *Journal fur reine und angewandte Mathematik* (Journal of pure and applied mathematics), and his 1931 paper "Über Funcktionen von Funcktionaloperatoren" (On functions of functional operators), which appeared in *Annals of Mathematics*, were two of a number of papers in which he more fully developed the properties of functions that manipulated vectors.

In his 1929 paper "Zur Algebra der Funcktionaloperatoren und Theorie der normalen Operatoren" (On the algebra of functional operators and the theory of normal operators), appearing in *Mathematische Annalen*, von Neumann introduced the concept of a ring of operators that later became known as a von Neumann algebra. With American mathematician Francis Murray he wrote a series of four papers titled "On Rings of Operators, I, II, III, IV," which appeared in *Annals of Mathematics* between 1936 and 1943. These articles explained how to decompose von Neumann algebras into sums of fundamental structures known as factors and to classify them into five different types. Functional analysts continue to regard highly this set of papers for its thorough development and elegant resolution of an unexpected set of properties.

Atomic Weapons and Nuclear Energy

As the United States prepared to enter World War II in the early 1940s, von Neumann changed the primary focus of his research from pure to applied mathematics. Having become a naturalized American citizen in 1937, he frequently worked as a scientist and a consultant for military and governmental organizations. He was a member of the Scientific Advisory Committee to the Ballistics Research Laboratories at Aberdeen Proving Ground in Maryland from 1940 to 1957, worked for the Naval Bureau of Ordnance in Washington, D.C., from 1943 to 1955, and served as a consultant to the Naval Ordnance Laboratory in Silver Spring, Maryland, from 1947 to 1955. Initially his responsibilities with all three organizations involved the computation of ballistics tables that indicated the distance an artillery weapon would fire its shell based on the gun's angle of elevation, the size of the charge, the wind speed, the air pressure, and other variable factors. In later years he participated in the design of computer hardware and the development of numerical techniques for solving additional problems with military applications.

In 1943 von Neumann became a consultant to the Los Alamos Scientific Laboratory where the government had assembled a large group of scientists to develop atomic weapons as part of the Manhattan Project. Von Neumann analyzed the constraints of spherical geometry that impacted the initial implosion required to create a sufficient amount of fissionable material in a coordinated manner. Borrowing time on several early computer systems, he devised and ran programs to analyze the hydrodynamics of shock waves and deterioration waves that would be created by such an explosion. He reported his research finding in internal documents such as the 1942 report "Theory of Detonation Waves," the 1944 report "Surface Water Waves Excited by an Underground Explosion," and the 1945 report "Refraction, Intersection and Reflection of Shock Waves." In July 1946, after atomic bombs were dropped on the Japanese cities of Hiroshima and Nagasaki, he was among the observers of the tests of nuclear bombs at the Bikini Atoll off the Marshall Islands in the Pacific Ocean. The following year he was awarded the Presidential Medal of Merit and the U.S. Navy's Distinguished Civilian Award in recognition of his work for the military during the war.

During the next five years von Neumann played a key role in the development of a new generation of bombs based on the principle of nuclear fusion. In "Los Alamos Scientific Laboratory Report LA-575," an internal technical report submitted in June 1946, he and Hungarian-born scientist Edward Teller recommended the development of a superbomb 1,000 times as powerful as the first atomic bomb. As a member of the U.S. Armed Forces Special Weapons Project from 1950 to 1955, a member of the U.S. Air Force's Scientific Advisory Board from 1951 to 1957, a member of the

General Advisory Committee to the Atomic Energy Commission from 1952 to 1954, and a consultant to the Los Alamos Scientific Laboratory from 1943 to 1955, von Neumann participated in both the scientific and political developments that led to the detonation of the first hydrogen bomb in November 1952.

Serving as chairman of the Advisory Committee on Guided Missiles from 1954 to 1957, a group that became known as the Von Neumann Committee, he helped to develop long-range missiles to deliver nuclear bombs to their targets. As a consultant to Oak Ridge National Laboratory in Tennessee from 1949 to 1954, a member of the Technical Advisory Panel on Atomic Energy from 1953 to 1957, and a member of the Atomic Energy Commission from 1954 to 1957, he also investigated the peacetime uses of atomic energy. He presented his ideas on aspects of the nuclear age in three articles from 1955: "Can We Survive Technology?" which appeared in *Fortune* magazine; "Defense in Atomic War," published in *The Scientific Basis of Weapons;* and "Impact of Atomic Energy on the Physical and Chemical Sciences," which appeared in *Technical Review.* In 1956, in recognition of his work on the development of nuclear weapons and atomic energy, he was awarded the Presidential Medal of Freedom, the Albert Einstein Commemorative Award, and the Enrico Fermi Award.

Computer Architecture and Numerical Analysis

During the 1940s and 1950s von Neumann made significant contributions to the design of computer hardware and the development of numerical algorithms for solving problems using computer programs. In 1944 he joined American computer pioneers J. Presper Eckert and John Mauchly and a group of researchers at the University of Pennsylvania's Moore School to work on the Electronic Numerical Integrator and Calculator (ENIAC), the first general-purpose electronic, digital computer. With Eckert and Mauchly he helped plan the Electronic Discrete Variable Automatic Computer (EDVAC), which incorporated several innovative design ideas. In 1945 von Neumann issued an internal document titled "First Draft of a Report on the EDVAC" that provided an outline of the components and the functioning of the proposed machine. This preliminary report introduced the concept of electronically storing a program of instructions in the computer's memory and allowing the computer to step through the execution of the program's commands without any intervention from its human operators. Although Eckert and Mauchly originated most of the concepts, the organizational structure presented in this report became known as von Neumann architecture. This architecture, consisting of five separate units for computation, logical control, memory, input, and output as well as the stored program concept, continues to be the basic design used in most nonparallel computers. Von Neumann and American mathematician and computer scientist Hermann Goldstine further elaborated on these design ideas in 1946 in an unpublished but widely circulated paper titled "The Principles of Large Scale Computing Machines."

Late in 1945 von Neumann severed his association with Eckert and Mauchly and initiated a project to build a computer at the

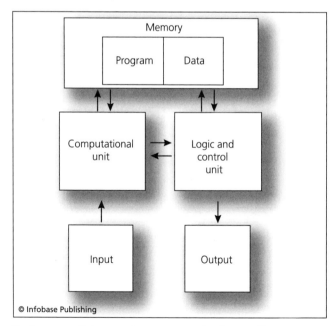

Most nonparallel computers are organized according to von Neumann architecture with five separate units for computation, logical control, input, output, and a memory in which both the program and the data are stored.

Institute for Advanced Studies (IAS). Completed in 1952 the IAS computer implemented all the design concepts of the von Neumann architecture and was used for experimental scientific research. As chairman of the National Research Council's Committee on High-Speed Computing (CHSC) from 1946 to 1952, he freely shared the details of the computer's design. Between 1952 and 1955, 17 laboratories around the world built copies of the IAS machine, including the RAND Corporation's JOHNNIAC computer, which was named after von Neumann.

In addition to his pioneering work with computer hardware, von Neumann developed innovative algorithms for performing numerical analysis on computers. In 1945 he introduced the merge sort algorithm in which the first and second halves of an array are each sorted recursively and then merged together. He devised methods of programming a computer to find eigenvalues, extreme values of functions of several variables, inverses of matrices, and the solutions of nonlinear partial differential equations. He developed general principles for stability analysis to ensure that the solutions generated by computers were not rendered unreliable by the propagation of errors due to the rounding off of numerical values and the use of approximation techniques.

Von Neumann's research on numerical techniques made significant contributions to the development of Monte Carlo methods, algorithms that use random statistical samples to generate approximate numerical solutions. In the paper that he presented at the 1949 Symposium on the Monte Carlo Method, "Various Techniques Used in Connection with Random Digits," he introduced the mid-square method for producing pseudo-random numbers. This method generates a sequence of eight-digit integers by squaring each entry and selecting the eight middle digits of the result as the next entry in the sequence. As reported in their 1950 paper "Statistical Statement of Values of First 2,000 Decimal Digits of e and π Calculated on the ENIAC," published in the CHSC's journal *Mathematical Tables and Other Aids to Computation*, von Neumann, Greek-American mathematician Nicholas Metropolis, and German-American computer scientist George W. Reitwiesner determined that the digits of π that they examined were randomly distributed, but the digits of e deviated significantly from a random pattern. In the 1955 article "Continued Fraction Expansion of $2^{\frac{1}{3}}$," which appeared in the same journal, von Neumann and American mathematician Bryant Tuckerman implemented the technique of continued fractions in a computer program to generate 2,000 partial quotients of the quantity $\sqrt[3]{2}$ and to analyze the randomness of the results. Von Neumann's work in numerical analysis encouraged other researchers to use computers to conduct empirical and theoretical investigations of random numbers and led to the wide use of Monte Carlo algorithms.

Automata Theory

Paralleling his work on the design of computer hardware, von Neumann developed an interest in the methods by which living organisms transfer and process information. He started by studying cellular automata, collections of cells on a grid whose evolution in iterative time steps is determined by the states of neighboring cells through a fixed set of rules. In 1946 he developed a self-replicating automaton and later experimented with automata that produced increasingly complex descendants. These unpublished projects culminated in his discovery of a universal constructor, an automaton that could encode both the information about its own structure and the method for replicating itself. He also used automata theory to investigate the possibility of designing reliable machines using unreliable components.

Von Neumann's earliest publication on the subject of automata was the 1951 paper "The General and Logical Theory of Automata," appearing in the monograph *Cerebral Mechanisms in Behavior*. This paper elaborated on the lecture "The Logic of Analogue Nets and Automata" that he had delivered at the Hixon Symposium in 1948 in Pasadena, California. When he died in 1957 von Neumann left two unfinished works on automata theory. In 1956 he had delivered the Silliman Lectures series at Yale University on the parallels between the workings of the human brain and digital computers. His unfinished summary of these lectures was published in 1958 as a book titled *The Computer and the Brain*. In 1966 his colleague Arthur Burks completed his draft manuscript on automata theory and published the book *Theory of Self-Reproducing Automata,* which detailed the concept of a universal constructor.

Throughout his career von Neumann received many honors in recognition of his diverse achievements. His two-part paper "Almost Periodic Functions and Groups," published in 1934 and 1935 in the *Transactions of the American Mathematical Society,* earned him the 1938 Bôcher Memorial Prize of the American Mathematical Society (AMS). The year before the AMS had selected him as the Colloquium lecturer at their annual national conference in 1937 and then in 1944 the AMS chose him as its Gibbs Lecturer. He later served as president of the AMS, from 1951 to 1952. In addition, seven national academies in Italy, Peru, the Netherlands, and the United States elected him to membership. On February 8, 1957, after a painful two-year battle with cancer that confined him to a wheelchair and then to a hospital bed, he died in Washington, D.C., at the age of 53.

Several organizations have established lasting tributes to von Neumann in recognition of his contributions to management science and computer technology. The Institute for Operations Research and Management Science annually awards the John von Neumann Theory Prize to an individual who has made fundamental and sustained contributions to the theories of operations research and the management sciences. In 1990 the Institute of Electrical and Electronics Engineers established the John von Neumann Medal as an annual award to recognize outstanding achievements in the field of computer technology. In 2005 the United States Post Office issued a commemorative stamp honoring him as an influential American scientist.

Conclusion

In an era when knowledge was becoming increasingly specialized, von Neumann contributed important and original ideas to many branches of mathematics, science, and technology. Physicists recognize his contributions to the establishment of an axiomatic basis for quantum mechanics. Economists appreciate his applications of game theory to their social science discipline. In computer technology the von Neumann architecture is recognized as the dominant model for the design of digital computers. Military leaders acknowledge his contributions to the development of atomic and nuclear weapons. Biological researchers have continued to develop his seminal ideas on self-replicating automata. Within the field of mathematics, von Neumann algebras continue to influence the study of operator theory. Because his research impacted so many disciplines John von Neumann is one of the most well-known mathematicians of the 20th century.

FURTHER READING

Aspray, William. *John von Neumann and the Origins of Modern Computing*. Cambridge, Mass.: MIT Press, 1990. Detailed biography focusing on his work with computers.

———. "The Mathematical Reception of the Modern Computer: John von Neumann and the Institute for Advanced Study Computer." In *Studies in the History of Mathematics*, edited by Esther R. Phillips, 166–194. Washington, D.C.: Mathematical Association of America, 1987. Discussion of von Neumann's work with early computers.

———. "The Transformation of Numerical Analysis by the Computer: An Example from the Work of John von Neumann." In *The History of Modern Mathematics, Volume II: Institutions and Applications*, edited by David E. Rowe and John McCleary, 307–322. Boston: Academic Press, 1989. Discussion of von Neumann's work with computer algorithms for random numbers and Monte Carlo methods.

Dieudonné, J. "Von Neumann, Johann." In *Dictionary of Scientific Biography*, Vol. 14, edited by Charles C. Gillispie, 88–92. New York: Scribner, 1972. Encyclopedic biography, including a detailed description of his writings in mathematics and computer science.

Heims, Steve J. *John von Neumann and Norbert Wiener: From Mathematics to the Technologies of Life and Death*. Cambridge, Mass.: MIT Press, 1980. Historical work contrasting the contributions of these two mathematicians to the development of technology with potential military applications.

James, Ioan. "John von Neumann." In *Remarkable Mathematicians from Euler to von Neumann*, 412–416. Washington, D.C.:

Mathematical Association of America, 2003. Brief biography and description of his impact on mathematics and computer science.

Lee, J. A. N. "John Louis von Neumann." The History of Computing. Available online. URL: http://ei.cs.vt.edu/~history/VonNeumann.html. Accessed September 1, 2005. Biography from the Department of Computer Science at Virginia Tech.

Lord, C. D. "John von Neumann, 1903–1957, Hungarian American Mathematician." In *Notable Mathematicians: From Ancient Times to the Present*, edited by Robyn V. Young, 491–494. Detroit, Mich.: Gale, 1998. Brief but informative profile of von Neumann and his work.

O'Connor, J. J., and E. F. Robertson. "John von Neumann." MacTutor History of Mathematics Archive, University of Saint Andrews. Available online. URL: http://www-groups.dcs.st-andrews.ac.uk/~history/Mathematicians/Von_Neumann.html. Accessed September 1, 2005. Biography from the University of Saint Andrews, Scotland.

Ulam, Stanislaw. "John von Neumann, 1903–1957." *Bulletin of the American Mathematical Society* 64 (1958): 1–49. One of eight articles in a special issue of this mathematics journal providing a biographical sketch of von Neumann and a review of his work.

von Neumann, John. *The Computer and the Brain.* New Haven, Conn.: Yale University Press, 1958. Book based on a week of lectures that he gave at Yale University about similarities and difference between the workings of the human brain and computers of the day.

von Neumann, John, and Oskar Morgenstern. *Theory of Games and Economic Behavior.* Princeton, N.J.: Princeton University Press, 2004. Sixtieth-anniversary edition of the seminal 1944 book upon which modern game theory is built.

Grace Murray Hopper

8

(1906–1992)

Navy commander Grace Murray Hopper programmed the Mark I computer, wrote the first compiler program, and formulated the essential ideas of the COBOL programming language. *(Bettmann/ CORBIS)*

Computer Software Innovator

Grace Murray Hopper left her position as a college mathematics professor to become one of the first programmers of the Mark I computer. She wrote the first compiler program to enable computers to assemble blocks of code from stored collections of routines. Her FLOW-MATIC software that used commands written in English became the basis for the widely-used COBOL programming language. Through her work for the United States Navy, her contacts with industry leaders, her publications, and her frequent conference presentations, she influenced the development and standardization of software for automated data processing. She helped to popularize the terms *computer bug* and *debugging* a computer program.

Early Life and Education

Grace Brewster Murray was born on December 9, 1906, in New York City. She was the oldest child of Walter Fletcher Murray, an insurance broker, and Mary Campbell Van Horne, the daughter of a civil engineer. An inquisitive child, she enjoyed building mechanical toys with a metal construction set and one day disassembled seven alarm clocks to examine their internal components. Her mother's love of mathematics and her father's determination to remain productive and self-sufficient despite a physical handicap influenced her outlook on life. Her parents ensured that Grace, her sister, Mary, and her brother, Roger, were well educated. Grace graduated from the Graham School and Schoonmakers School, two private institutions for girls in New York City, and spent a college preparatory year at Hartridge School in Plainfield, New Jersey. In addition to studying mathematics and science, she enjoyed participating in sports, playing music, and acting.

In 1924 Murray entered Vassar College in Poughkeepsie, New York, as a mathematics and physics major. In addition to completing her required coursework in the arts and sciences, she tutored students in physics and audited classes in botany, physiology, geology, business, and economics. During her senior year she was inducted into Phi Beta Kappa, the oldest collegiate honor society in the United States. When she graduated with a bachelor's degree in mathematics and physics in 1928 she earned a Vassar College Fellowship to attend Yale University in New Haven, Connecticut. Two years later she received her master's degree in mathematics from Yale. In June 1930 she married Vincent Foster Hopper, an English instructor at New York University's School of Commerce.

In 1931 Grace Murray Hopper accepted a position as a mathematics instructor at Vassar College for the modest salary of $800 per year. She taught courses in algebra, geometry, trigonometry, calculus, probability, statistics, analysis, and mechanical drawing. While teaching at Vassar she continued her graduate coursework and mathematical research at Yale, earning a Ph.D. in mathematics in 1934. Under the direction of algebraist Øystein Ore, she wrote a doctoral dissertation titled "New Types of Irreducibility Criteria" that investigated conditions under which a polynomial could be written as the product of two simpler polynomials. Her dissertation earned her induction into Sigma Xi, the international scientific research honor society, and a promotion to the rank of associate professor. In 1936 the *American Mathematical Monthly* published her paper "The Ungenerated Seven as an Index to Pythagorean Number Theory." After 10 years of teaching, she spent the academic year 1941–42 taking advanced courses and conducting additional research as a Vassar Faculty Fellow at the Courant Institute of New York University.

Programming and Debugging the Mark Series of Computers

When the United States entered World War II in December 1943, Hopper attempted to enlist in the U.S. Navy. At 36 years of age, standing five feet six inches tall and weighing 105 pounds, the navy rejected her as overage and underweight. The navy further advised her that they were unwilling to approve her application because they considered her work as a mathematics professor to be crucial to the war effort. Hopper took a leave of absence from her teaching duties at Vassar and convinced a recruiter to accept her into the Women Accepted for Voluntary Emergency Service (WAVES), the women's branch of the U.S. Naval Reserve. At the end of June 1944, she graduated first in her class from the United States Naval Reserve Midshipman's School for Women in Northampton, Massachusetts, and was commissioned a lieutenant junior grade. Five days later she reported for duty under the direction of Howard Aiken at the Bureau of Ordnance Computation Project at Harvard University in Cambridge, Massachusetts.

Seven years earlier, Aiken, a navy commander and a Harvard mathematics and physics professor, had proposed the design of an automatic calculating machine. From 1939 to 1943 he worked with engineers from the university and the company International Business Machines (IBM) to build the Automatic Sequence Controlled Calculator (ASCC) at the IBM laboratories in Endicott, New York. In January 1944, after testing the computer, IBM disassembled it, moved it to Harvard, and donated it to the university, where it was leased by the navy for the remainder of the war. The Mark I, as the first American-made, large-scale, automatically sequenced digital computer was known, weighed five tons, had 750,000 parts, used 530 miles of wire, and stood eight feet high, eight feet wide, and 51 feet long. The Mark I's 3,300 electromechanical relays enabled it to perform three additions per second with 23 significant digits of precision.

Hopper's first assignment was to program the computer to calculate the coefficients of the arc tangent series for the computation of self-propelled rocket trajectories. Her responsibilities as a programmer required her to translate computational algorithms and formulas into binary coded computer instructions that were fed into the computer on punched paper tape. Most of the programs she created and ran calculated ballistics tables that indicated the distance an artillery weapon would fire its shell based on the gun's angle of elevation, the size of the charge, the wind speed, the air pressure, and other variable factors. She also wrote programs to calculate the area cleared by a minesweeping detector towed behind a ship. Hopper, Aiken, and a staff of eight navy personnel kept the Mark I running programs 24 hours a day for a variety of military applications, including determining the tensile strength of steel plates, analyzing the propagation of radio waves, and simulating the shock wave that would result from the explosion of an atomic bomb.

During her first year in Aiken's lab, Hopper wrote a manual to describe the process of programming the Mark I. The 561-page manual provided a detailed description of the function of each of the computer's assemblies and circuits as well as samples of programs to accomplish a variety of tasks. Published in 1946 under the title *A Manual of Operation for the Automatic Sequence Controlled Calculator*, Hopper's handbook became the first of 35 volumes in the *Annals of the Computation Laboratory of Harvard University*.

As the staff at the Computation Laboratory grew, Hopper assumed responsibility for overseeing all the programming of the computer and for training the new programmers. Since programmers who were writing code in the machine language of zeros and ones needed to understand the functioning of the hardware at its most basic level, she created a timing chart for the electromechanical relays, accompanied by circuit diagrams to show the sequencing of the operations within the machine. In a collection of notebooks she recorded segments of code to calculate square roots, evaluate trigonometric functions, sum collections of numerical values, and perform other fundamental tasks that might be reused in later programs. She encouraged each programmer to collect a similar library of code segments and to share his or her routines with coworkers to reduce coding errors and eliminate redundant effort.

While continuing to program, operate, and maintain the Mark I, Hopper and her colleagues at the Computation Laboratory built its successor, the Mark II. By mid-1945 the machine was operational and was performing arithmetic operations five times faster than its predecessor. On September 9, 1945, when the Mark II stopped running, she and a team of programmers discovered a moth trapped between two of its 17,000 relays. They removed the insect with tweezers and pasted it into the logbook with the notation that they had "debugged" the machine. Although Harvard personnel had previously used the term *bug* to describe problems with computing machines, Hopper's frequent recounting of this episode popularized the use of the terms *computer bug* and the *debugging* of a computer. She extended the use of the terminology to software problems where "debugging a program" described the process of fixing errors of logic or syntax in the instructions fed to a computer. In 1946 the navy awarded Hopper its Naval Ordnance Development Award for her work on the Mark series of computers.

After the war ended Hopper left active military duty, resigned her faculty position at Vassar, and joined the U.S. Naval Reserve. She accepted a three-year fellowship to continue to work from 1946 to 1949 as a civilian research fellow in engineering systems and applied physics at Aiken's Computation Laboratory at Harvard. With Aiken she coauthored a three-part paper titled "The Automatic Sequence Controlled Calculator. I, II, III," which appeared in 1946 in the journal *Electrical Engineering*. The first installment described the Mark I's mechanisms and the processes that accomplished addition and subtraction. In the second part of the paper, they explained how the computer performed the more involved operations of multiplication and division. The final piece described the preparation and planning of the punched tapes that fed the programming instructions into the computer.

To encourage open discussion of computers and computing in the young but growing industry, Hopper and Aiken organized and ran the first international conferences on computing. Their January 1947 "Symposium on Large Scale Digital Calculating Machinery" at Harvard attracted an audience of 300 representatives from laboratories and research groups in universities, industry, and government. Two years later they ran a second conference that attracted a larger and more international audience. Appreciating the importance of communication and collaboration with colleagues, Hopper continued to organize and participate in many similar endeavors throughout her career.

Hopper's primary responsibilities at the Computation Laboratory were to direct a new staff of civilian programmers writing code for military, scientific, and commercial applications in areas such as atomic physics, radio waves, optics, and astronomy. Typical work included a contract for the U.S. Air Force to calculate and produce 14 volumes of tables containing values of Bessel functions for use in applications involving electronics and radar. In 1948 Hopper and her colleagues wrote one of the first commercial data processing programs that computed premiums and dividends, calculated interest on loans, and printed customers' bills for Prudential Life Insurance Company. This successful program validated her contention that computers could be used widely in business, an opinion that most of her contemporaries in the computer field did not share at the time.

Between 1946 and 1948 the staff at Computation Laboratory designed and built a third computer named Mark III. This electronic machine, which used vacuum tubes instead of electromechanical relays, performed calculations 50 times as fast as the Mark I. The Mark III used magnetic tape made of paper with a metallic coating instead of paper tape with punched holes to feed programs and data into the computer. In August 1948, after Hopper and her staff of programmers succeeded in coding and running a variety of test programs for the machine, it was delivered to the air force.

Compilers and COBOL Programming

In 1949 Hopper accepted a position as senior mathematician with Eckert-Mauchly Computer Corporation (EMCC) in Philadelphia. She remained at the company for 18 years, through its 1950 purchase by Remington Rand and its 1955 merger with Sperry Corporation. Computer pioneers John Mauchly and J. Presper Eckert had established EMCC in 1947 after leaving the Moore School at the University of Pennsylvania, where they had helped to develop the Electronic Numerical Integrator and Calculator (ENIAC). As EMCC's first project, Mauchly and Eckert designed and built the Binary Automatic Computer (BINAC) under a contract with Northrup Aircraft Corporation. Hopper learned to program the machine in octal notation using the symbols 0, 1, 2, . . ., 7, a modest advance beyond the more primitive binary machine language of zeros and ones. In 1951 Remington Rand introduced the Universal Automatic Computer (UNIVAC), the first mass-produced, commercial computer. With its electronic vacuum tubes, metal tapes, and magnetic core memory, UNIVAC operated 1,000 times as fast as Mark I and could process both numeric and alphabetic data.

While working on programming techniques for the UNIVAC, Hopper played a key role in conceiving, developing, and implementing the concept of a compiler, a word she introduced to describe a program that enabled a computer to build programs from smaller blocks of code. She stored in the computer's memory a library of subroutines—segments of code that instructed the computer to perform specific functions—and assigned each subroutine a three-letter mnemonic code. In 1952 she produced the first compiler, a program known as A-0 that automatically assembled and sequenced the collection of subroutines indicated in the coded instructions supplied to it. The resulting program assembled by the computer then ran as a unit. In May 1952, at a conference at Mellon Institute in Pittsburgh sponsored by the Association of Computing Machinery, Hopper presented her ideas on compilers in a paper titled "The Education of a Computer." Her computing colleagues were hesitant to embrace her radical ideas about teaching a machine to do a substantial portion of its own programming.

As director of automatic programming development at the UNIVAC Division, Hopper persisted in her work to develop new compilers and to popularize their use. She helped to organize and publicize navy seminars on automatic computing at which she served as master of ceremonies. She explained the principles of compiling in her 1953 paper "Compiling Routines," which appeared in *Computers and Automation.* With Mauchly she coauthored the paper "The Influence of Programming Techniques on the Design of Computers," published in 1953 in the *Proceedings of the Institute of Radio Engineers.* In 1953 she convinced DuPont Chemical Company, the U.S. Census Bureau, the U.S. Navy, and the U.S. Air Force to adopt the A-2, a commercial compiler that she had created. By 1956, when UNIVAC introduced MATH-MAGIC, Hopper's next compiler, the computing industry had embraced the concept. Designed to compete with IBM's Formula Translation (FORTRAN), MATH-MAGIC enabled programmers to write programs for scientific applications using instructions that included verbs in English and mathematical symbols.

In addition to developing the A-series of algebraic compilers for scientific applications, Hopper created a B-series of business compilers for data processing. Although her supervisors had rejected her 1953 proposal to develop an English-language compiler for business applications, she had continued to work on the project. In January 1955 she presented an internal report titled "The Preliminary Definition of a Data Processing Compiler" and demonstrated a prototype compiler that used commands such as *Input, Compare, Go To, Transfer, If Greater, Jump, Rewind,* and *Output* to process files of inventory and pricing information. She also ran the program with the same instructions written in French and German to impress upon her supervisors the machine's flexible capabilities. Her successful demonstration convinced Sperry Rand Corporation to provide resources to develop the product. By the end of 1956 her B-0, or FLOW-MATIC, compiler that allowed the computer to recognize 20 English words and phrases as commands had been adopted by U.S. Steel, Westinghouse, DuPont, Lockheed, the U.S. Navy, and the U.S. Air Force for payroll, billing, and inventory control. Hopper and the members of her group visited clients' businesses to provide training in the use of the software. Programmers were able to learn to use FLOW-MATIC after two weeks of training, and the English-language commands that it employed reduced their programming and debugging time by a factor of four.

In 1957 when IBM introduced Commercial Translator (COMTRAN) and Honeywell Corporation introduced Fully Automated Compiling Technique (FACT), Hopper and other leaders in the computing industry recognized the need to develop standardized computer languages that would run on any manufacturer's machine. She helped to organize a 1959 meeting at the Pentagon in Washington, D.C., where leaders of industry, government, and universities agreed to collaborate on the development of a uniform data processing language. To coordinate the massive project they formed an executive committee known as Conference on Data Systems Languages (CODASYL) under the leadership of air force colonel Charles Phillips. As a special adviser to CODASYL, Hopper became an influential member of a small group who established the forms and procedures that defined the work of the body. In 1960 the Short-Range Committee produced a first version of Common Business Oriented Language (COBOL). Since many of the committee's members were UNIVAC clients, they incorporated the majority of the design features of Hopper's FLOW-MATIC compiler into this new high-level programming language.

Hopper worked with her programming group at the UNIVAC Division to implement the COBOL language on their computer. On December 6, 1960, UNIVAC and RCA publicly announced that they had produced commercial versions of the COBOL programming language. That day Hopper and her group ran a test COBOL program on their UNIVAC II. The following day the same program ran on an RCA 501 computer and produced identical results. The highly publicized demonstration proved that standardization of programming languages could be achieved, resulting in a separation between high-level software and the particular hardware platform on which the program was to be run. COBOL achieved Hopper's goal of creating a readable language using English commands that was portable from one machine to another. In her remaining years at UNIVAC, she helped to create standard manuals and tools for the language that became the most widely used high-level computer language.

In addition to developing FLOW-MATIC and influencing the development of COBOL in direct ways, Hopper maintained a busy schedule of conference appearances at which she shared her vision for the future of computing with colleagues from industry, the government, the military, and education. Typical of her presentations were the lecture "Automatic Programming in Business and Industry," which she delivered at the 1958 Electronics Data Processing Conference; the talk titled "Automatic Programming Language and Programming Aids," which she gave at the 1959 Computers for Artillery Conference; and the speech "A Data-Processing Compiler," which she presented at the 1959 meeting of the National Machine Accountants Association.

Hopper's increasing visibility and her accomplishments within the computer field led to her recognition by numerous organizations. The navy promoted her to lieutenant commander in 1952 and to the rank of commander in 1959. In 1962 she became one of the first two women to be named fellows of the Institute of Electrical and Electronics Engineers. The following year she was elected a fellow of the American Association for the Advancement of Sciences. In 1964 the Society of Women Engineers honored her with its Achievement Award. UNIVAC promoted her to become director of research in systems and programming in 1961 and to senior staff scientist in 1964.

Return to Active Duty in the Navy

In 1966 the navy informed 60-year-old Hopper that since she had served in the U.S. Naval Reserves longer than 20 years, its regulations mandated that she retire at the end of the year. In August 1967, after a seven-month retirement, the navy recalled her to temporary active duty that lasted until 1986. Her initial assignment was to standardize computer programming languages for all nonweaponry navy computers. As director of the Navy Programming Languages Group at the Pentagon, she was responsible for ensuring that all hardware vendors who provided computers to the navy complied with the standards for COBOL that were issued by the America National Standards Institute (ANSI). Working with industry leaders, she helped produce a COBOL certifier, a detailed test computer program that determined whether a particular company's implementation of COBOL complied with all the requirements of the ANSI standard. She also developed translator programs to convert nonstandard COBOL languages into the standardized version. In 1971 Hopper and her group produced a manual for training and reference titled *Fundamentals of COBOL* that was distributed to all navy computer contractors to assist them in the implementation of standard COBOL on their machines.

Recognition of Hopper's service to the navy and her contributions to the field of computer science came from many organizations. The Data Processing Management Association named her its 1969 "Computer Science Man of the Year." In 1973 she was promoted to the rank of captain by a special act of Congress because she was too old to be promoted through the navy's regular process. That same year she was elected a member of the National Academy of Engineering, received the Legion of Merit, and became the first American and the first woman to be elected a Distinguished Fellow of the British Computer Society.

After a reorganization of navy hierarchy in 1977, Hopper became a member of the Naval Data Automation Command in Washington, D.C. In this capacity she was responsible for advising on the adoption of new technology and producing annual reports assessing the navy's use of computer technology. She recommended the use of networks of microcomputers rather than centralized main frames and the implementation of changes to make the navy's data processing installations more efficient. In addition to fulfilling her military responsibilities, she lectured on management sciences at George Washington University and in 1984 coauthored the college textbook *Understanding Computers* with Steven Mandell. The navy promoted her to the rank of commodore in 1983 and the rank of rear admiral two years later. In 1985 she wrote a chapter titled "Future Possibilities: Data, Hardware, Software, and People" for the book *Naval Tactical Command and Control.* That same year the navy named their new data processing center in San Diego, California, the Grace Murray Hopper Service Center. In 1986 Hopper received the Defense Distinguished Service Medal, the highest award given by the Department of Defense, and retired at the age of 79 as the oldest military officer on active duty.

Before the year ended, Hopper joined Digital Equipment Corporation (DEC) as a senior consultant. From 1986 to 1990 she represented DEC at computer industry forums and other speaking engagements, making as many as 200 presentations each year on advanced computing concepts and the value of information and data. During her talks she often gave members of the audience a piece of wire 11.8 inches long, the distance an electrical signal can travel in a nanosecond (a billionth of a second), and showed them a coil of wire 1,000 times longer representing a microsecond (a millionth of a second) to remind them not to waste time. She told her audiences that she kept a clock in her office that ran counterclockwise to encourage people to think in nonstandard ways. One of her frequently repeated recommendations was that it is easier to apologize than to ask permission for pursuing a good idea. In 1991 she was awarded the National Medal of Technology, the nation's highest honor in engineering and technology. On January 1, 1992, she died in her sleep at her home in Alexandria, Virginia, at the age of 85. She was buried with full military honors in Arlington National Cemetery, in Virginia.

Conclusion

The woman who was called "Amazing Grace," the "Grandmother of the Computer Age," the "Grand Lady of Software," and "Grandma COBOL" influenced the evolution of computer programming during the first 40 years of the computer age. Her introduction of compilers to select and sequence blocks of code from a stored library of subroutines radically changed the way computer programmers approached their work. Through her FLOW-MATIC compiler and her work with CODASYL, she influenced the formulation and implementation of a portable, English-like, standardized COBOL programming language for business uses. Her work for the navy and its industrial contractors helped standardize military and commercial data processing software and policies.

FURTHER READING

Billings, Charlene W. *Grace Hopper: Navy Admiral and Computer Pioneer.* Hillside, N.J.: Enslow Publishers, 1989. Biography and discussion of her work with computer programming; intended for younger audiences.

Danis, Sharron Ann. "Rear Admiral Grace Murray Hopper." The History of Computing. Available online. URL: http://ei.cs.vt.edu/~history/Hopper.Danis.html. Accessed September 1, 2005. Biography from the Department of Computer Science at Virginia Tech.

King, Amy C., and Tina Schalch. "Grace Brewster Murray Hopper." In *Women of Mathematics: A Biobibliographic Sourcebook*, edited by Louise S. Grinstein and Paul J. Campbell, 67–73. New York: Greenwood Press, 1987. Biographical profile with an evaluation of her contributions and an extensive list of references.

Koch, Laura Coffin. "Grace Brewster Murray Hopper." In *Notable Women in Mathematics: A Biographical Dictionary*, edited by Charlene Morrow and Teri Perl, 80–85. Westport, Conn.: Greenwood Press, 1998. Short biography of Hopper.

Norman, Rebecca. "Grace Murray Hopper." Biographies of Women Mathematicians. Available online. URL: http://www.agnesscott.edu/lriddle/women/hopper.htm. Accessed September 1, 2005. Biography provided by Agnes Scott College in Atlanta, Georgia.

O'Connor, J. J., and E. F. Robertson. "Grace Brewster Murray Hopper." MacTutor History of Mathematics Archive, University of Saint Andrews. Available online. URL: http://www-groups.dcs.st-andrews.ac.uk/~history/Mathematicians/Hopper.html. Accessed September 1, 2005. Biography with additional links from the University of Saint Andrews, Scotland.

Williams, Katherine. *Grace Hopper: Admiral of the Cyber Sea.* Annapolis, Md.: Naval Institute Press, 2004. Authoritative biography researched from published and unpublished sources.

————. "Grace Hopper, 1906–1992, American Computer Scientist." In *Notable Mathematicians: From Ancient Times to the Present,* edited by Robyn V. Young, 252–255. Detroit, Mich.: Gale, 1998. Brief but informative profile of Hopper and her work.

Alan Turing

9

(1912–1954)

Alan Turing decrypted German military codes during World War II and formulated the concept of a theoretical Turing machine that established the basic design principles for multipurpose computers. *(Time & Life Pictures/ Getty Images)*

Father of Modern Computing

Alan Turing (pronounced TOUR-ing) helped to design and build some of the earliest electromechanical and electronic computers. His formulation of the concept of a theoretical Turing machine resolved the decision problem in mathematical logic and established the basic design principles for multipurpose computers. During World War II he used his knowledge of statistics, cryptography, and logic to design machines that deciphered German military codes. He developed the Turing test to determine if a machine possessed artificial intelligence. His pioneering work with computer hardware and software earned him the title "Father of Modern Computing."

Education and the Central Limit Theorem

Alan Mathison Turing was born on June 23, 1912, in the Paddington section of London, England, to Julius Mathison Turing, a member of the Foreign Civil Service, and Ethel Sara Stoney. Alan and his older brother, John, were raised in London by Colonel and Mrs. Ward, a retired military couple, while their parents lived in India. The boys attended London's public schools, joining their parents for annual vacations in Wales, Ireland, Scotland, France, and Italy. When their father retired in 1926, their parents settled in the resort town of Dinard on the northern coast of France and sent Alan and John to Sherborne School, a public boarding school for boys in Dorset on the southern coast of England. During his five years at the school, Alan won prizes for excellence in mathematics, conducted independent chemistry experiments, and became interested in chess and competitive running. After the death of his classmate Christopher Morcom in 1930, he became interested in metaphysical questions about the human mind that became central to his research on computers later in his life.

In 1931 Turing won a scholarship to attend King's College at Cambridge University, where he focused his studies on mathematics. He joined the university's Moral Science Club, and in December of his third year he read a paper titled "Mathematics and Logic" at one of the organization's meetings. His paper presented the argument that mathematics had a variety of interpretations and could not be reduced to an application of pure logic. In 1934, at the end of his three-year undergraduate program of studies, his performance as one of the top nine students on the three-part mathematical examination known as the Tripos merited the distinction "B-Star Wrangler" and earned him a £200 stipend to continue his education as a research scholar for an additional year of graduate studies.

During the final year of his undergraduate program and his year of his graduate work, Turing became interested in probability and statistics. In the fall semester of 1933 he attended a series of lectures on the methodology of science in which astrophysicist Sir Arthur Stanley Eddington discussed the fact that experimental measurements subject to observational errors tend to have an approximately normal, or Gaussian, distribution. Unsatisfied with Eddington's informal motivation of this phenomenon, Turing developed a rigorous mathematical proof of the fundamental principle that is now known as the central limit theorem for independent random variables. Although Finnish mathematician Jarl Waldemar Lindeberg had proven the result 12 years earlier, Turing's 1934 paper titled "On the Gaussian Error Function" earned him election as a fellow of King's College in 1935, a master's degree in mathematics from the college later that year, and the university's Smith's Prize as the best paper in mathematics the following year.

Introduction of the Turing Machine

During the two-year period from 1935 to 1937, Turing's work focused on the question of decidability. In 1931 Austro-Hungarian mathematician Kurt Gödel had shown that there were mathematical statements that could not be proved. Three years earlier German mathematician David Hilbert had posed the related question known as *Entscheidungsproblem* (the decision problem) that asked if there existed an algorithm for deciding whether a given mathematical statement could be proved. Hilbert regarded this question as the principal problem of mathematical logic because an algorithm for the decision problem could be used to determine whether any given mathematical statement was true. In his paper "On Computable Numbers, with an Application to the *Entscheidungsproblem*," which appeared in 1937 in the *Proceedings of the London Mathematical Society*, Turing demonstrated that no such algorithm existed.

Turing's paper introduced an abstract machine now known as a Turing machine that moved from one state to another based on the symbols it scanned and the state it was in. He described a tape of infinite length that was divided into squares, each of which could contain a single symbol. His theoretical machine could recognize

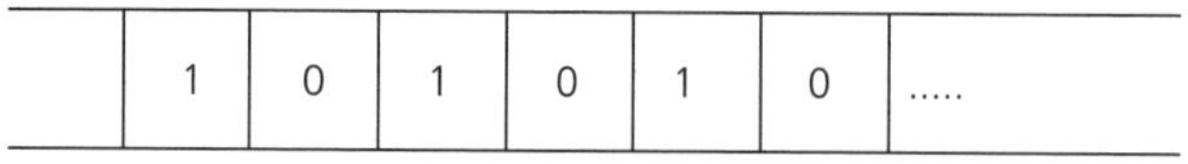

	ꟾ	0	1
S0	0, S1, right	1, S1, right	No change, S1, right
S1	1, S0, left	No change, S0, right	0, S0, left

The top tape shows:

1	0	1	0	1	0	.....

A Turing machine consists of a tape of infinite length and a finite set of instructions that determine the action to be performed when presented with any combination of state and character. The six rules listed in the operation table for this Turing machine will start with a blank tape and produce the infinite sequence ıoıoıoıoıo ... that represents the binary expansion of a computable number. The instructions in row S0 and column ꟾ indicate that if the machine is in state o and the current symbol is a blank, then it should write the symbol o, change to state ı, and move the tape one square to the right.

the symbol in the current square of the tape; erase it, replace it, or leave it alone; change its state; and move to the preceding or subsequent square on the tape to process another symbol. The actions performed by the machine when it encountered each symbol were predetermined by a finite set of rules known as its operation table. Each instruction was expressed as a set of five characters representing the current state, the current symbol, the erase/replace action, the new state, and the left/right movement. If there was no instruction corresponding to the current state and symbol, the machine would halt its operation.

Using his abstract machine Turing introduced two rigorous definitions that enabled him to provide the answer to the decision problem. He formally specified an algorithm as a finite set of instructions that could be carried out by a Turing machine. He also defined a real number between zero and one to be a computable number if there was some Turing machine that would start with a blank tape and produce the number's binary expansion as an infinite sequence of zeros and ones. For example, the binary expansion 1101000 ... represented the quantity given by the infinite sum

$$\frac{1}{2} + \frac{1}{2^2} + \frac{0}{2^3} + \frac{1}{2^4} + \frac{0}{2^5} + \frac{0}{2^6} + \frac{0}{2^7} + \cdots .$$ Using these definitions Turing

proved that there could be no algorithm to determine if any given Turing machine produced an infinite sequence of zeros and ones without halting. By showing that the truth of the statement "This Turing machine produces a computable number" could not be determined by a finite algorithm, he demonstrated that the answer to the decision problem was "No."

Although Turing completed his work on this paper in April 1936, it did not appear in print until January 1937 because American mathematician Alonzo Church had arrived at the same conclusion in his paper "An Unsolvable Problem in Elementary Number Theory," which appeared in April 1936 in the *American Journal of Mathematics*. Church had used the concept of λ-definability (lambda-definability) to prove the existence of an algorithmically unsolvable problem. As they read each other's papers, the two mathematicians realized that they had independently resolved the decision problem by different methods. Turing proved the equivalence of their results in his paper "Computability and λ-Definability," which appeared in 1937 in the *Journal of Symbolic Logic*, a publication that Church had founded the previous year. Their independently discovered results became known as the Church-Turing thesis.

In addition to solving the decision problem, Turing's paper on computable numbers introduced the concept of a universal Turing machine, a multipurpose computer that could perform the functions of any automatic calculating device when supplied with the proper algorithm. He suggested that by reading "description numbers" fed to it on a tape, the multipurpose machine could be programmed to perform any set of computations or automatic sequence of operations. The universal Turing machine detailed in this paper served as a model for the first working computers.

In September 1936 Turing sailed to the United States to spend a year conducting research with Church at Princeton University in New Jersey. He received one of three Procter Visiting Fellowship's from Cambridge University to stay for a second year and finish his doctoral degree under Church's supervision. In 1938 he completed a dissertation titled "Systems of Logic Based on Ordinals," which was published the following year in the *Proceedings of the London Mathematical Society*. His thesis in the area of mathematical logic examined the solvability of questions within a logical system $L\alpha$

that had been constructed from an ordinal number α. The ideas he presented in this paper influenced the work of other mathematicians during the subsequent two decades. Polish mathematician Emil Post, who had independently developed a concept equivalent to the Turing machine, drew on Turing's thesis work in the early 1940s as he developed a system for classifying problems according to degrees of unsolvability. In the late 1950s Austrian mathematician Georg Kreisel expanded on Turing's use of ordinal logics to characterize informal methods of proofs.

In addition to his thesis research Turing completed other work in algebra, number theory, and boolean logic during his stay in Princeton. His paper "Finite Approximations to Lie Groups" that appeared in 1938 in *Annals of Mathematics* discussed methods for constructing a mathematical structure known as a finite group that possessed most of the properties of a related but more complicated Lie group. Another paper titled "The Extensions of a Group" that was published in the same year in *Compositio Mathematica* (Compilation of mathematics) gave a more efficient, general method to obtain some results on group extensions that German mathematician Reinhold Baer had derived. Turing pursued an idea for attacking the Riemann hypothesis, one of the leading open problems in number theory, by attempting to mechanically calculate the values of the Riemann zeta function. His continuation of this work after leaving Princeton led to the paper "A Method for the Calculation of the Zeta-Function," which he completed in 1939, although it was not published until 1943 in the *Proceedings of the London Mathematical Society*.

When he left Princeton after receiving his doctorate in 1938, Turing returned to King's College to resume his fellowship. He brought with him electromechanical relays that he had built in the graduate student machine shop in Princeton's Physics Department. These electrical switches corresponded to the logical operations of "and," "or," and "not" and physically implemented the systems of equations known as logic gates that Turing and his colleagues had sketched out on paper. They had combined banks of these components to build the first three stages of an electrical calculator that could multiply numbers. In 1938 Turing secured a grant of £40 to build a special-purpose analog computer using his electromechanical relays to compute values of the Riemann zeta function. He never completed this project because World War II moved his career in other directions.

Deciphering German Naval Codes

On September 4, 1939, one day after the outbreak in Europe of World War II, Turing reported to the Government Code and Cipher School at Bletchley Park in Buckinghamshire, where he joined the cryptanalytic unit of the secret Ultra project charged with breaking German military codes. The Germans had developed a cipher machine called the Enigma that used three rotating wheels, each with 26 settings and a plugboard with 26 holes to scramble the letters of the alphabet, creating a cipher code that had more than a trillion combinations. Building on the work that a group of Polish mathematicians had done to decode systematically messages sent using an earlier, more primitive version of the Enigma machine, Turing and his colleagues successfully built machines to decode messages being sent to German U-boats stationed in the North Atlantic Ocean.

Turing contributed to the work of the cryptanalytic unit in several ways. He helped build decoding machines using electromechanical relays that methodically tested key codes until they found the correct combination. The machines, which were called "Bombes" after the ticking sound produced by the opening and closing of the relays, reduced the time required for decoding a message from weeks to hours. Turing also used his knowledge of statistics to develop new statistical decoding techniques that employed sequential analysis, empirical methods, and the logarithms of the weight of evidence. In 1940 he wrote a classified internal document on the Enigma titled *Mathematical Theory of ENIGMA Machine*, known at Bletchley Park as the "Prof's Book." In November 1941 Turing, who had risen to a position of leadership within the organization, wrote directly to Prime Minister Winston Churchill requesting additional trained staff members. Recognizing the importance of their work as part of the secret Ultra project, Churchill instructed his staff to make this request a priority. By the end of 1941 the Bombes had become so successful that the British were decoding German naval messages within minutes after they were sent. This increased level of military intelligence about U-boat operations made the shipping lanes in the North Atlantic much safer for commercial and military convoys.

In 1943, when the Germans introduced a new coding machine known as the Lorenz and a new coding system known as Fish, the British and U.S. intelligence units collaboratively designed and built the first operational electronic computer. The Colossus used 1,500 electronic vacuum tubes that were 1,000 times faster than the Bombes' electrical relays. The machines incorporated most of Turing's design ideas from the slower Bombes and employed many of his combinatorial and statistical algorithms that had contributed to the Bombes' success. By early 1944 the Colossus was successfully deciphering messages encrypted by the Lorenz machine. In 1945, in recognition of the vital role he had played in the war effort, the British government awarded Turing the Order of the British Empire.

In addition to his work at Bletchley Park, Turing spent part of his time during the war years producing research papers on mathematical logic and consulting with U.S. computer designers and cryptanalysts. In 1941 he wrote a three-part unpublished manuscript titled "Some Theorems about Church's System." The following year the *Journal of Symbolic Logic* published the related papers "A Formal Theorem in Church's Theory of Types," which he had coauthored with his former Cambridge University professor Maxwell Newman, and "The Use of Dots as Brackets in Church's System." This group of papers contributed several refinements to Church's system of λ-calculus that became a valuable tool for computer scientists. At the end of 1942 Turing made a five-month trip to the United States where he visited Eastman Kodak Corporation, Bell Laboratories, National Cash Register Corporation, IBM, the Naval Computing Machine Laboratory, and the navy's cryptanalytic service, Communications Supplementary Activities (Washington), to share ideas about the decoding of messages and the building of computers.

ACE and MADAM Computer Projects

During the first five years after the war, Turing played a central role in the development of two computer projects. In June 1945 he declined the offer of a lectureship at Cambridge University to join the staff of the Mathematical Division of the National Physical Laboratory (NPL) in London, a government foundation established to design and build a multipurpose computer. Based on his work with the Bombes, Turing designed an electronic computing machine known as the Automatic Computing Engine (ACE). His design incorporated many fundamental features of modern computers, including internally stored instructions, random access memory, microprogramming, and the use of stacks to implement subroutine calls. In March 1946 he submitted a proposal titled "Proposed Electronic Calculator" for building the ACE. The report specified the complete description of the computer, including a logical circuit diagram and a cost estimate of £11,200. He envisioned the proposed computer as a physical implementation of his universal Turing machine, capable of being programmed to play chess and solve puzzles as well as decode messages and perform numerical calculations. In lectures to the Ministry of Supply in December 1946 and January 1947 and to the London

After World War II, Turing designed the Automatic Computing Engine (ACE) that incorporated many fundamental features of modern computers, including internally stored instructions, random access memory, microprogramming, and the use of stacks to implement subroutine calls. *(The Image Works)*

Mathematical Society in February 1947, he described his plans for ACE and his vision of machines that could be programmed to learn, would be permitted to make mistakes, and would display true intelligence. Frustrated by the bureaucracy and politics that delayed the project's approval for a year and prevented engineering work from beginning for an additional year, Turing resigned from the NPL in 1948. Two years later the laboratory successfully built a scaled-down version of his original proposal known as the Pilot ACE and subsequently produced a commercial model known as DEUCE.

At Newman's invitation Turing accepted an appointment to the faculty of Manchester University in 1948, where he became deputy director of the newly formed Royal Society Computing Laboratory. This group of mathematicians and scientists designed and built the Manchester Automatic Digital Machine (MADAM). Turing contributed to the design of the computer's software, developing standardized methods for writing the subroutines from which larger programs were built and writing programs that enabled the computer to accurately perform numerical analysis. In a paper titled "Rounding-Off Errors in Matrix Processes" that appeared in 1948 in the *Quarterly Journal of Mechanics and Applied Mathematics*, he discussed some of the limitations of programs that manipulated arrays of numbers. At the June 1949 EDSAC Inaugural Conference that introduced Cambridge University's newest computer, the Electronic Delay Storage Automatic Calculator (EDSAC), he presented a paper titled "Checking a Large Routine" in which he explained a systematic method for determining the correctness of a computer program. He supervised the production of *The Programmer's Handbook for the Manchester Electronic Computer*, which was published in 1950 at the Manchester University Computing Laboratory. Turing explained additional details about programming techniques for MADAM in his paper titled "Local Programming Methods and Conventions," which he presented at the 1951 Manchester University Computer Inaugural Conference. In 1951, in recognition of his pioneering work with computers and his development of the Turing machine, he was elected a fellow of the Royal Society.

Turing Test for Artificial Intelligence

As he had stated in his 1947 address to the London Mathematical Society, Turing's ultimate vision for computers was to design and build a machine that displayed true intelligence. During the 1947–48 academic year, he studied neurology and physiology at Cambridge University to further develop his understanding of the workings of the human brain. In the 1948 report "Intelligent Machinery" that he wrote for NPL, he elaborated on his idea of a thinking computer. His major publication on the subject was the 1950 paper "Computing Machinery and Intelligence," which appeared in the journal *Mind*. In this paper he proposed an experiment to determine if a computer possessed artificial intelligence. In his "imitation game," now known as the Turing test, a person typing at a keyboard sent questions to and received responses from a remote source. The experiment required the individual to determine whether the respondent at the other end of the conversation was a human or a computer. Turing predicted that within 50 years computers would be able to play this game so well that after five minutes of questioning, human interrogators would be able to identify correctly their remote correspondents only 70 percent of the time. The Turing test continues to be used as a measure of a computer's acquisition of artificial intelligence.

Turing directed his work on artificial intelligence to the general public in order to generate wide support for governmental funding of research on computers. In 1951 and 1952 he broadcast the radio programs titled "Can Digital Computers Think?" and "Can Automatic Calculating Machines Be Said to Think?" for the British Broadcasting Corporation. He contributed a section titled "Chess" to the chapter "Digital Computers Applied to Games" that appeared in the 1953 book *Faster Than Thought*. His comments emphasized that the ability to develop decision-making strategies in games like chess demonstrated some of the essential qualities of human intelligence. In his 1954 article "Solvable and Unsolvable Problems" that appeared in *Science News*, he presented to a general audience some insights into the limitations of computers' abilities to solve problems.

Mathematical Ideas in Biological Growth

In the early 1950s Turing became interested in applications of mathematical theory to morphogenesis, the development of patterns and forms in living organisms. Although he wrote several manuscripts on the subject, his only published work was the 1952 paper "The Chemical Basis of Morphogenesis" in the *Philosophical Transactions of the Royal Society*. In this paper he analyzed the mathematical phenomenon whereby small variations in the initial conditions of the differential equations that described the growth of an organism could result in significant variations in the organism's long-term development and behavior. He argued that this property accounted for asymmetrical developments in organisms as they adapted to their surroundings. Using this thesis, he attempted to explain the development of stripes and spots on the skins of animals and of phyllotaxis, the arrangement of leaves on plants. Turing's unpublished writings on morphogenesis included "Outline of the Development of the Daisy"; "A Diffusion Reaction Theory of Morphogenesis in Plants," written with British biologist Claude W. Wardlaw; and the three-part treatise "Morphogen Theory of Phyllotaxis" that included sections titled "Geometrical and Descriptive Phyllotaxis," "Chemical Theory of Morphogenesis," and "A Solution of the Morphogenetic Equations for the Case of Spherical Symmetry."

While working on the subjects of artificial intelligence and morphogenesis, Turing continued to conduct research in pure mathematics. In his paper "The Word Problem in Semigroups with Cancellation," published in 1950 in the *Annals of Mathematics*, he investigated the existence of an algorithm to determine if a given combination of algebraic elements was equal to the identity element of their algebraic structure. Post had proven that no such algorithm existed for structures known as semigroups; Turing was able to show that the same result applied to semigroups that satisfied an additional condition known as the cancellation law. In his 1953 paper "Some Calculations of the Riemann Zeta-Function," which appeared in the *Proceedings of the London Mathematical Society*, Turing implemented ideas that he had outlined in the late 1930s by using computing machines to calculate values of the Riemann zeta function.

In 1952 Turing was arrested for being a homosexual and was convicted of violating British law against gross indecency. He lost his security clearance, was sentenced to a year's probation, and was subjected to treatments with the female hormone estrogen. On June 7, 1954, while working on an electrolysis experiment involving potassium cyanide, he ingested a fatal dose of the toxic chemical. Police officials who found cyanide on the half-eaten apple next to his body ruled his death a suicide.

Conclusion

During his diverse career Alan Turing worked as a pure mathematician, a computer engineer, and a computer scientist. His introduction of the Turing machine provided a solution to the decision problem in mathematical logic. He built electromechanical relays, helped to design special-purpose computers called the Bombe and the Colossus for decrypting coded messages, and designed the multipurpose ACE computer. As a computer scientist, he developed programming techniques for the MADAM computer and introduced the Turing test for artificial intelligence. He applied his knowledge of many branches of mathematics—statistics, cryptography, group theory, number theory, and logic—to develop algorithms for deciphering codes, to study the morphogenesis of living organisms, and to analyze the Riemann zeta function.

In 1966 the Association for Computing Machinery, the international professional society of computer scientists, established the annual A. M. Turing Award to honor computer scientists and engineers for outstanding contributions to the field of computer science. By naming their highest award for Turing, the association recognized the importance of his work in articulating the mathematical foundation and the limits of computing. His pioneering work with both computer hardware and software, as well as his vision of the future of computers, merit his designation as the "Father of Modern Computing."

FURTHER READING

Breaking the Code. VHS, Video Treasures, 1997. Ninety-minute videorecording reenacting significant events in Turing's life. Coproduced by The Drama House and WGBH Boston for BBC North, based on Hugh Whitemore's play by the same name.

Davis, Martin. "Mathematical Logic and the Origin of Modern Computers." In *Studies in the History of Mathematics*, edited by Esther R. Phillips, 137–165. Washington, D.C.: Mathematical Association of America, 1987. Essay summarizing Turing's work in the foundations of modern computing.

Henderson, Harry. "Alan Turing (1912–1954)." In *Modern Mathematicians*, 88–101. New York: Facts On File, 1996. Biographical sketch with a discussion of his mathematics.

Hodges, Andrew. The Alan Turing Home Page. Available online. URL: http://www.turing.org.uk/turing. Accessed September 1, 2005. Extensive online collection of manuscripts, pictures, and other biographical information by Dr. Andrew Hodges of Wadham College, Oxford University.

———. *Alan Turing: The Enigma*. New York: Walker, 2000. Biography that includes a discussion of his mathematics.

O'Connor, J. J., and E. F. Robertson. "Alan Mathison Turing." MacTutor History of Mathematics Archive, University of Saint Andrews. Available online. URL: http://www-groups.dcs.st-andrews.ac.uk/~history/Mathematicians/Turing.html. Accessed August 31, 2005. Biography from the University of Saint Andrews, Scotland.

Simon, Joel. "Alan Turing, 1912–1954, English Algebraist and Logician." In *Notable Mathematicians: From Ancient Times to the Present*, edited by Robyn V. Young, 479–482. Detroit, Mich.: Gale, 1998. Brief but informative profile of Turing and his work.

Van Rootselaar, B. "Turing, Alan Mathison." In *Dictionary of Scientific Biography*, Vol. 13, edited by Charles C. Gillispie, 497–498. New York: Scribner, 1972. Encyclopedic biography, including a detailed description of his mathematical writings.

Paul Erdös

10

(1913–1996)

Paul Erdös collaborated with 500 research partners to write 1,500 books and papers in graph theory, combinatorics, set theory, and number theory. (*Courtesy of Fan Chung*)

Traveling Research Partner

During a career that spanned seven decades, Paul Erdös (pronounced AIR-dish) wrote more than 1,500 research papers with more than 500 mathematical partners. Without a formal appointment at any academic institution, he traveled the world giving guest lectures and visiting colleagues to discuss their common mathematical interests. His collaborative approach to conducting joint research was influential in changing the way that mathematicians work. Erdös made significant contributions to graph theory, combinatorics, and set theory and helped establish Ramsey theory, probabilistic number theory, and extremal theory as new branches of mathematics. His most important discoveries occurred in number theory in which he developed new proofs of theorems about prime numbers, abundant numbers, products of consecutive integers, and sequences of integers. His colorful language, unique personality, and wealth of intriguing problems made him a celebrity in the international mathematical community.

Brilliant Childhood

Paul Erdös was born on March 26, 1913, in Budapest, Hungary, to Jewish parents Lajös and Anna Wilhelm Erdös. His sisters, Magda and Klára, died during an epidemic of scarlet fever a few days before he was born. A year later, during World War I, the Russian army took his father prisoner and sent him to a work camp for six years. Raised as an only child, he was isolated by his mother's protective care. Doting on Paul's every need, his mother did so many things for him that he was 11 years old before he learned to tie his own shoes and 21 when he first buttered his own bread. Even as an adult he relied heavily on the assistance of friends and colleagues, as he had never learned to cook or to drive a car.

As the son of two high school math teachers, Erdös spent much of his childhood in the world of mathematical ideas. He learned to do simple arithmetic by the time he was two years old. At the age of three he understood the idea of negative numbers, once announcing to his mother that 100 minus 250 was "150 below zero." At the age of four he could multiply four-digit numbers in his head. After being tutored at home for most of his childhood, Erdös enrolled at Szent István Gimnásium, the high school where his father taught. There he competed with his classmates to solve the problems that appeared in the monthly magazine *Középiskolai Matematikai Lapok* (*KöMaL*; Mathematical journal for secondary schools). His picture and his solutions to these challenging problems appeared in several issues of *KöMaL* between 1926 and 1930. Although he was skilled at making computations and solving problems, Erdös was even more fascinated by proofs, the logical arguments that explained why mathematical properties are true. By the age of 17 he knew 37 proofs of the Pythagorean theorem, the famous result from geometry that relates the lengths of the three sides of a right triangle.

First Research Papers

At the end of high school, Erdös placed as the top-scoring student on the standardized college entrance exam and chose to attend Pázmány Péter Tudományegyetem, the national university in Budapest that provided advanced education in mathematics and science for the most talented young men and women in Hungary. He made friends with a group of students who often met by a statue in the park or went for a hike in the countryside to work on math problems and proofs. Sometimes Erdös would sit completely still while deep in thought. When an insightful idea came to his mind, he would leap up, flap his arms, and walk around with a burst of energy. He and his friends would discuss his idea to see if it helped to solve the problem or prove the theorem.

As an 18-year-old college freshman, Erdös discovered a new proof of a mathematical property that had been proven 80 years earlier by the Russian mathematician Pafnuty Chebyshev. The theorem involved prime numbers, or whole numbers greater than one that cannot be divided by any other positive numbers except themselves and one. Chebyshev had proven that for any number n that is greater than 1, there must be at least one prime number between n and $2n$. For example, between $n = 5$ and $2n = 10$ there is the prime number 7. Between 13 and 26 there are the primes 17, 19, and 23. Chebyshev had given a long explanation using some advanced mathematical ideas to prove that this result is true. Erdös found a proof that was much shorter and easier to understand. He also extended the theorem by showing that if $n \geq 7$, there are at least two primes of the form $4k + 1$ and $4k + 3$ between n and $2n$. László Kalmár, a mathematics professor at the University of Szeged, translated Erdös's proof into German and submitted it to his university's journal, *Acta Litterae Scientiarum Szeged* (Literary and scientific achievements at Szeged). The paper, "Beweis eines Satzes von Tschebyscheff" (Proof of a theorem of Tschebyscheff [Chebyshev]), published in 1932, was the first of 1,521 research papers that Erdös wrote during his long and productive mathematical career.

The next year Erdös discovered a new proof of a theorem that number theorists James Sylvester and Issai Schur had proven about the distribution of abundant numbers. A positive number n is abundant if its factors, the smaller numbers that divide it, add up to more than n. For example, 12 is abundant because its factors 1, 2, 3, 4, and 6 add up to more than 12. Erdös explained his proof in the paper "A Theorem of Sylvester and Schur," which was published in 1934 in the *Journal of the London Mathematical Society*. Schur was so impressed with Erdös's work that he called him the "Magician from Budapest." These two papers earned him a Ph.D. in mathematics.

Joint Research Collaborations

The circle of friends with whom Erdös discussed mathematics in the park had a lasting impact on the way he conducted his research throughout his professional life. In 1934 Erdös and Paul Turán published a joint paper titled "On a Problem in the Elementary Theory of Numbers" in the *American Mathematical Monthly*. In the same year he and George Szekeres wrote a paper, "Über die Anzahl der Abelschen Gruppen gegebener Ordnung und über ein verwandtes zahlentheoretisches Problem" (On the number of abelian groups of a given order and on a related number theoretic problem), that was published in the journal *Acta Litterae Scientiarum Szeged*. Esther Klein discovered a property about the arrangement of five points that were randomly placed on a piece of paper. As she, Erdös, and Szekeres worked to generalize this result to larger numbers of points, Klein and Szekeres fell in love with each other and eventually married. In 1935 Erdös and Szekeres wrote a paper titled "A Combinatorial Problem in Geometry" for the journal *Compositio Mathematica* (Compilation of mathematics) presenting their work on this problem, which Erdös informally named the "Happy End Problem."

During his career Erdös wrote papers with more than 500 research partners. These enthusiastic collaborations influenced the way mathematicians do their work. When he published his first research paper in 1932, only 10 percent of articles published in mathematical journals were authored by more than one person.

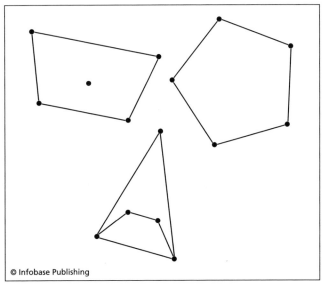

The "Happy End Problem" states that for any set of five points in a plane, if no three of the points are collinear (lie on a straight line) then four of the points form a convex four-sided polygon.

Most mathematicians worked by themselves and did not communicate their work to one another until they had successfully proven a theorem. Seventy years later more than 50 percent of research papers in the field are coauthored. Mathematicians routinely discuss their unfinished ideas with one another and work together to prove theorems. Although Erdös is not solely responsible for this change, he had a greater impact than any other single individual.

As an interesting amusement, each mathematician has acquired an Erdös number that indicates how close he or she came to working with the prolific collaborator. Erdös's own Erdös number is zero. Each of the approximately 500 mathematicians who wrote papers with him has Erdös number one. The almost 6,000 mathematicians who wrote a paper with one of Erdös's coauthors but did not write a paper with Erdös have Erdös number two. People who wrote papers with them have Erdös number three, and so on. The fact that most living mathematicians have an Erdös number less than 10 indicates how central Erdös has been to the joint efforts of modern mathematical research.

Traveling Mathematician

After completing his doctoral work at Pázmány in 1934, Erdös obtained a research fellowship at the University of Manchester, in England. During his four-year appointment at Manchester, he made so many trips to visit colleagues at other European universities that he was never in the same city for more than a few weeks at a time, a practice that he continued throughout his career. These collaborations produced 46 research papers, mostly in number theory. The *Journal of the London Mathematical Society* published 16 of these papers, including "On the Density of Some Sequences of Numbers" (1935), "On the Representation of an Integer as the Sum of k kth Powers" (1936), "On the Sum and Difference of Squares of Primes" (1937), and "On the Number of Integers Which Can Be Represented by a Binary Form" (1938).

Erdös's most influential works during this period were two results in extremal theory, a new branch of mathematics. In the 1938 paper "On Sequences of Integers No One of Which Divides the Product of Two Others and on Some Related Problems," published in the Russian journal *Miteilungen Forschun—Institut der Mathematik und der Mechanik Univität Tomsk* (Research communications—Institute of Mathematics and Mechanics, University of Tomsk), Erdös used techniques from graph theory to solve a problem in number theory. Building on this innovative strategy, Turán developed extremal theory in which mathematicians investigate questions such as: How many edges can a graph have before it must include at least one triangle? That same year Erdös, Chinese mathematician Chao Ko, and German mathematician Richard Rado proved the Erdös-Ko-Rado theorem, which immediately became one of the fundamental results in extremal theory even though it was not published until 1961 in the *Quarterly Journal of Mathematics, Oxford Series* under the title "Intersection Theorems for Systems of Finite Sets." As this branch of mathematics developed, Erdös's many contributions helped to identify the major questions and provided new problem-solving strategies.

In 1938, when Europe was on the brink of World War II, Erdös fled to the United States, where he obtained a one-year appointment as a mathematical researcher at the Institute for Advanced Study in Princeton, New Jersey. Inspired by Polish mathematician Mark Kac's visiting lecture, he applied techniques of probability to solve problems in number theory. The two mathematicians discovered that for any positive integer n, the number of prime divisors of the integers less than n has a normal distribution. This important result, known as the Erdös-Kac theorem, appeared in their paper "The Gaussian Law of Errors in the Theory of Additive Number Theoretic Functions" in 1940 in the *American Journal of Mathematics*. This paper established a new area of mathematics known as probabilistic number theory and introduced techniques called Erdös methods.

While at the institute, Erdös also proved that the product of consecutive integers can never be a square. This result typified the kind of problems that he identified and solved throughout his career—deep results that were easy to state but difficult to prove. His two papers on this topic, "Note on the Product of Consecutive Integers. I, II," were published in 1939 in the *Journal of the London Mathematical Society*.

From 1940 to 1954 Erdös held brief appointments at the University of Pennsylvania, Purdue University, the University of Michigan, and the University of Notre Dame but was often not affiliated with any particular institution. Teaching an organized course for four months to a group of students did not interest him; he preferred to travel throughout North America giving guest lectures for a fee and visiting the homes of mathematical colleagues. At each new location he engaged in intense research sessions for several days at a time. During this period of his career, Erdös produced an average of 40 research papers annually and gained approximately 20 new research partners each year. Traveling lightly he carried one suitcase containing a single change of clothes, a shopping bag filled with copies of research papers, and a notebook in which he scribbled new ideas. He communicated with his international network of colleagues by sending more than 1,000 letters and postcards each year. When he arrived at the home of a mathematician for one of his brief visits, he would greet them with his famous saying "Another roof, another proof."

Diverse Mathematical Contributions

With his research collaborators and in his independent research, Erdös made significant contributions to many branches of mathematics and helped to develop new areas of investigation. His 1942 paper "On the Law of the Iterated Logarithm," published in the *Annals of Mathematics*, made an important contribution to number theory. With Alfred Tarski he produced the first study of inaccessible cardinal numbers, a result that is fundamental to modern set theory. Their work appeared in the paper "On Families of Mutually Exclusive Sets," published in 1943 in the *Annals of Mathematics*. In combinatorics, the mathematics of counting, he proved many results about partitions—the number of ways to write a positive number as the sum of other positive numbers—such as writing 4 as 4 or 3+1 or 2+2 or 2+1+1 or 1+1+1+1. His 1973 book *The Art of Counting* contains a collection of his most influential papers on this subject. In geometry he wrote about the ways to cut up a square into pieces, each of which is a different sized square. He helped to popularize lesser known areas of mathematics, such as Ramsey theory in which mathematicians study the occurrence of patterns in random collections of data.

Erdös introduced the probabilistic method to graph theory by showing the existence of a graph having certain Ramsey properties. Without constructing such a graph, he proved that there was a positive probability that a random graph satisfying a particular set of conditions would have these properties. His influential paper "Some Remarks on the Theory of Graphs," published in 1947 in the *Bulletin of the American Mathematical Society*, gave the first use of the probabilistic method, a technique that researchers in discrete mathematics and in theoretical computer science still use.

In 1949 Erdös made the most significant discovery of his career when he and the Norwegian mathematician Atle Selberg discovered an elegant proof of the prime number theorem. This famous result from number theory states that for any large, positive integer n, the number of primes less than n is approximately $\dfrac{n}{\ln n}$. Adrien-Marie Legendre of France and Carl Friedrich Gauss of Germany had proposed the theorem around 1800; Frenchman Jacques Hadamard and Charles de la Vallée-Poussin of Belgium had given elaborate proofs in 1896. Working independently, Erdös and Selberg proved two theorems that together produced a simple proof of the famous theorem. Their accomplishments were celebrated by the mathematical community but were tarnished by controversy when each one accused the other of stealing his work. When the dispute was settled, Selberg was awarded the prestigious 1950 Fields Medal, the international award recognizing a significant accomplishment by a mathematician under the age of 40, and Erdös received the 1951 Frank Nelson Cole Prize in Number Theory, the American Mathematical Society's award for the best paper in number theory. Erdös's contribution appeared in the paper "On a New Method in Elementary Number Theory Which Leads to an Elementary Proof of the Prime Number Theorem," published in 1949 in the *Proceedings of the National Academy of Sciences.*

Eccentric Genius

At different times in his life, Erdös's ability to travel to certain countries was severely limited. During the 1940s World War II prevented him from visiting his family and friends in eastern Europe. From 1954 to 1963 the U.S. government refused to allow him to enter the country. In August 1941 he had been arrested with English mathematician Arthur Stone and Japanese mathematician Shizuo Kakutani for trespassing at a military radar installation on Long Island in New York. Government officials cited this incident and his friendships with people in Communist countries as evidence that he posed a threat to national security. Until his passport was restored, Erdös made frequent trips to Canada where his American colleagues would meet with him to do their collaborative research.

Throughout his life Erdös had a very close relationship with his mother. For 20 years she maintained a collection of his research papers, sending copies to colleagues who requested them. Each summer she vacationed with him at a guesthouse at the Hungarian Academy of Sciences, where she met many of his research partners. From 1964 until her death in 1971, she was his constant travel companion. After she died, Ron Graham and Fan Chung, two mathematicians from AT&T Bell Labs in New Jersey who wrote dozens of papers with Erdös, assumed many of the responsibilities that she had fulfilled for him. They forwarded his mail, updated his visa, made sure his taxes were paid, and arranged his transportation. They eventually built an addition onto their house so Erdös could have a bedroom, bathroom, and library to use as his home a few weeks each year.

With others managing the necessary details of his life, Erdös devoted every possible minute to his mathematics. He usually awoke at 5:00 in the morning and worked for 19 hours, taking only brief naps during the day. At times three groups of mathematicians gathered in his hotel room, each working on a different problem. In the style of a chess master, Erdös moved from group to group helping to produce proofs of all three theorems simultaneously. When he had surgery to repair a cataract in one eye, he asked the doctors to allow him to read with the other eye during the operation. They refused his request but did permit a mathematician to be present in the operating room so Erdös could productively use the time discussing mathematics. At a conference in Kalamazoo, Michigan, in 1996, Erdös collapsed and was rushed to the hospital, where doctors implanted a pacemaker to regulate his heart. He persuaded the doctors to accompany him to the conference that evening so he could attend the banquet as scheduled.

Known as a generous colleague, Erdös shared his time and the little money that he had with mathematically talented students. In 1984 when he won the $50,000 Wolf Prize for mathematical achievement, he donated $30,000 to establish a scholarship fund at the university Technion in Israel and gave away most of the remaining money, keeping only $720 for himself. He often rearranged his traveling schedule to meet with promising students, offering prizes for the solutions to an assortment of problems. The prizes ranged in value from $10 for the solution of an elementary problem to $3,000 for a difficult problem that would likely require years of work. During a casual conversation at dinner, he might write down 10 problems that would keep his guest busy for the next few years.

During his lifetime Erdös developed a collection of colorful sayings that others referred to as "Erdös-ese." When he was ready to discuss mathematics, he would tell his friends "My brain is open." He referred to a child as an "epsilon," the letter of the Greek alphabet that mathematicians usually use to represent a small quantity. Women were "bosses," and men were "slaves." When talking politics, he called the Soviet Union "Joe," after the Communist dictator Joseph Stalin, and the United States "Sam," after Uncle Sam. A person "arrived" when they were born and "left" when they died. A stupid law was "trivial," and a mathematician who had stopped doing research was "dead." He did not care for music or alcohol, which he called "noise" and "poison." He did love coffee and drank many cups of it while trying to prove theorems; in fact, he often said that a mathematician was a machine for turning coffee into theorems.

Erdös believed that mathematics was as much an art as it was a science. He did not think that it was acceptable to simply prove that a result was true; he wanted the proof to be creative, insightful, and well designed. He took more pride in creating an elegant proof than he did in discovering a new result by a tedious method. Many of his research papers, including his first paper on Chebyshev's theorem and his proof with Selberg of the prime number theorem, were beautiful proofs. He joked that the "Supreme Fascist" (his name for God) had a collection called "The Book," which contained the best proof of each mathematical result. When he discovered or learned of an ingenious proof, he would say that it was "straight from The Book."

Erdös frequently thought and talked about his death. When he was still a teenager, he often expressed concern that he was becoming a frail old man and was worried that he would soon die. He joked that, since the world was thought to be 2 billion years old when he was a child but scientists now estimated that it was 4.5 billion years old, that change made him a 2.5 billion-year-old man. When he was 55, he started to refer to himself as Paul Erdös, P.G.O.M., which stood for "Poor Great Old Man." Every five years he added more letters until he was Paul Erdös, P.G.O.M. L.D.A.D.L.D.C.D., meaning "Poor Great Old Man, Living Dead, Archaeological Discovery, Legally Dead, Counts Dead." The last two letters were a reference to the Hungarian Academy of Sciences whose members were no longer counted on the official roster after their 75th birthday.

On September 20, 1996, while visiting Warsaw, Poland, for a graph theory workshop, Erdös suffered a heart attack in his hotel room, was brought to the hospital, and died at the age of 83. For many years prior to his death, mathematicians had been honoring him for his contributions to mathematics. Fifteen universities had awarded him honorary degrees and eight national academies of science had inducted him as a member. Mathematicians had organized many international conferences and had published collections of research papers in celebration of his birthday. After his death, Graham and Chung published a list of all the unsolved Erdös problems in graph theory and promised to pay the prize money for their solutions. Andrew Beal, a banker and amateur mathematician from Texas, created a fund to pay for the solutions of the Erdös problems in the other areas of mathematics.

Conclusion

The 1,521 mathematical research papers that bear Paul Erdös's name make him the most prolific researcher and writer in the history of mathematics. His having written nearly 1,100 of these papers with at least one other research partner helped mathematicians recognize the benefits of working collaboratively. He made significant contributions to established branches of mathematics such as number theory, combinatorics, graph theory, and set theory and helped develop new areas such as extremal theory, probabilistic number theory, and Ramsey theory. He was one of a handful of researchers who defined 20th-century mathematics.

FURTHER READING

Babai, Laszlo, and Joel Spencer. "Paul Erdös (1913–1996)." *Notices of the American Mathematical Society* 45 (1998): 64–73. Article in mathematics journal providing a detailed description of his work, some biographical information, and a list of references.

Cook, Jane Stewart. "Paul Erdös, 1913–1996, Hungarian Number Theorist." In *Notable Mathematicians: From Ancient Times to the Present,* edited by Robyn V. Young, 161–163. Detroit, Mich.: Gale, 1998. Brief but informative profile of Erdös and his work.

Csicsery, George Paul. *"N Is a Number: A Portrait of Paul Erdös."* VHS, 1993; DVD, 2004. Documentary film about his life and work.

Erdös, Paul. *The Art of Counting.* Boston: MIT Press, 1973. A large collection of his classic papers on number theory.

Hoffman, Paul. *The Man Who Loved Only Numbers: The Story of Paul Erdös and the Search for Mathematical Truth.* New York: Hyperion, 1998. Detailed biography describing his life and works.

O'Connor, J. J., and E. F. Robertson. "Paul Erdös." MacTutor History of Mathematics Archive, University of Saint Andrews. Available online. URL: http://www-groups.dcs.st-andrews.ac.uk/~history/Mathematicians/Erdos.html. Accessed July 15, 2004. Biography from the University of Saint Andrews, Scotland.

Schechter, Bruce. *My Brain Is Open: The Mathematical Journeys of Paul Erdös.* New York: Simon and Schuster, 1998. Detailed biography describing his life and works.

GLOSSARY

absolutely normal number A real number whose digits occur with equal frequency in every number base.

abundant number An integer such as 12 that is less than the sum of its factors. Also known as an over-perfect number.

aleph The first letter of the Hebrew alphabet, used in set theory to denote different orders of infinity such as $\aleph_0$ (aleph-zero), the cardinality of the natural numbers, and $\aleph_1$ (aleph-one), the cardinality of the real numbers.

algebra The branch of mathematics dealing with the manipulation of variables and equations.

algebraic equation A mathematical statement equating two algebraic expressions.

algebraic expression An expression built up out of numbers and variables using the operations of addition, subtraction, multiplication, division, raising to a power, and taking a root.

algebraic geometry The branch of mathematics concerned with the study of the roots of polynomial equations.

algebraic number A real number that is the root of a polynomial equation with integer coefficients.

algebraic topology The branch of mathematics in which groups of functions are used to study the properties of geometrical surfaces. Also known as analysis situs.

algorithm A precise set of instructions for solving a problem.

analysis See FUNCTIONAL ANALYSIS.

analysis situs See ALGEBRAIC TOPOLOGY.

area The amount of surface space occupied by a two-dimensional object.

arithmetic The study of computation.

artificial intelligence The ability of a computer to simulate human reasoning and behavior.

astronomy The scientific study of stars, planets, and other heavenly bodies.

automaton An object, organism, or system whose evolution in iterative time steps is determined by its interaction with neighboring objects, organisms, or systems under a fixed set of rules.

axiom A statement giving a property of an undefined term or a relationship between undefined terms. The axioms of a specific mathematical theory govern the behavior of the undefined terms in that theory; they are assumed to be true and cannot be proved. Also known as a postulate.

Bernoulli number A sequence of fractions that occur in many applications in number theory and analysis.

binary form A polynomial with two variables in which every term has the same degree.

binary notation A method used by digital computers to represent a number as a sum of powers of two using only the digits 0 and 1.

binomial coefficient A positive integer given by the computation

$$\binom{n}{k} = \frac{n!}{k! \cdot (n-k)!},$$ where n and k are integers satisfying $0 \le k \le n$.

biquadratic form An algebraic operator related to polynomials in which the exponents in every term add up to four.

Brownian motion The rapid movements of pollen and other organic particles suspended in water.

calculus The branch of mathematics dealing with derivatives and integrals.

calculus of variations The branch of mathematics in which one searches for functions that satisfy a set of differential equations and that minimize the value of a related expression.

cardinality A numerical value giving the size of a set.

cardinality of the continuum A numerical value giving the size of the set of real numbers in the unit interval [0, 1].

cellular automaton A collection of cells on a grid whose evolution in iterative time steps is determined by the states of neighboring cells through a fixed set of rules.

chaos theory   The branch of mathematics that studies the orderly patterns that occur in seemingly random situations and mathematical systems in which small changes in initial conditions result in significant variations in outputs.

circle   The set of all points in a plane at a given distance (the radius) from a fixed point (the center).

circumference   (1) The points on a circle. (2) The measure of the total arc length of a circle; it is 2π times the radius of the circle.

COBOL   Common Business Oriented Language, the computer programming language developed in the 1950s that uses English words as instructions to perform data processing tasks.

coefficient   A number or known quantity that multiplies a variable in an algebraic expression.

combinatorics   The branch of mathematics concerned with techniques of counting.

commutative   The algebraic property of a collection of objects in which two objects combined in one order produce the same results as the same two objects combined in the opposite order.

compiler   A computer program that enables a computer to build programs by selecting and sequencing smaller blocks of code from a library of subroutines.

complete   The property of a set of axioms that is satisfied when every theorem in the discipline follows as a logical consequence of the axioms.

complex number   A number that can be written as the sum of a real number and the square root of a negative real number.

composite number   A positive integer that can be factored as the product of two or more primes.

computable number   A real number between zero and one whose binary expansion as an infinite sequence of zeros and ones can be produced by some Turing machine that starts with a blank tape.

computer program   A set of instructions that controls the operation of a computer.

consistent   The property of a set of axioms that is satisfied when no combination of axioms lead to a contradiction.

continuum hypothesis   The principle of set theory stating that every infinite subset of real numbers is either countable or has the cardinality of the continuum.

coordinates   The numbers indicating the location of a point on a plane or in a higher-dimensional space.

cosine   For an acute angle in a right triangle, the ratio of the adjacent side to the hypotenuse.

countable   An infinite set is countable if it can be put into a one-to-one correspondence with the set of natural numbers.

cryptography   The study of coding and decoding secret messages.

cube   (1) A regular solid having six congruent faces, each of which is a square. (2) To multiply a quantity times itself three times; raise to the third power.

cubic   (1) A polynomial of degree three. (2) An equation or curve (graph) corresponding to a cubic polynomial.

cybernetics   The branch of science concerned with the study of the interactions between humans and machines.

debug a computer program   To find and fix errors of logic or syntax in the instructions fed to a computer.

decimal notation   A method using the digits 0, 1, 2, ... , 9 to represent a number as a sum of powers of 10.

degree   (1) A unit of angle measure equal to $\frac{1}{360}$ of a circle. (2) The number of edges that meet at a vertex in a polygon or polyhedron. (3) The sum of the exponents of all the variables occurring in a term of a polynomial or algebraic expression.

degree of a polynomial or equation   The highest exponent occurring in any of its terms.

derivative   A function formed as the limit of a ratio of differences of the values of another function. One of two fundamental ideas of calculus that indicates the rate at which a quantity is changing.

diameter   (1) The distance across a circle. (2) A line segment of this length passing through the center of a circle joining two points on opposite sides of the circle.

differential equation   An equation involving derivatives.

differentiation   The process of determining the derivative of a function.

Diophantine analysis   The branch of number theory dealing with methods for finding integer solutions to polynomial equations.

Dirichlet problem The determination of functions that have well-behaved derivatives in a given region and that take specified values on its boundary.

divisible A number is divisible by another if the resulting quotient has no remainder.

divisor See FACTOR.

e A naturally occurring constant whose value is approximately 2.71828.

Elements The influential book on geometry and number theory written by Euclid of Alexandria.

encryption The process of translating a message into a secret code.

Enigma machine A special-purpose computer with rotating wheels and a plugboard used by the German military during World War II to send and receive coded messages.

entire function A function whose derivative is defined for all complex numbers.

equation A mathematical sentence stating that two algebraic expressions or numerical quantities have the same value.

equilateral A property of a polygon that is satisfied when all sides are equal in length.

ergodic Dealing with quantities whose values are governed by probability.

Euclidean geometry The mathematical system of geometry derived from the five postulates assumed by Euclid of Alexandria.

even number An integer that can be written as two times another integer.

exponent A number indicating how many repeated factors of the quantity occur. Also known as power.

extrapolation A numerical technique to predict the future values associated with a phenomenon based on observations of past behavior.

extremal theory The branch of mathematics concerned with the minimum conditions that an object must satisfy to guarantee that a particular property holds.

factor An integer that divides a given integer without leaving a remainder. Also known as a divisor.

Fourier series An infinite series whose terms are of the form a_n $\sin(nx)$ and $b_n \cos(nx)$.

fractal A recursively defined geometrical object in which each section of the pattern is similar to the entire design.

fraction See RATIONAL NUMBER.

functional analysis The branch of mathematics dealing with the investigation of properties of sets of functions. Also known as analysis.

game theory The mathematical study of competition and cooperation.

geometry The mathematical study of shapes, forms, their transformations, and the spaces that contain them.

graph theory The branch of mathematics in which relationships between objects are represented by a collection of vertices and edges.

group theory The branch of abstract algebra dealing with the structure, properties, and interaction of groups (sets of objects that can be combined with an operation that satisfies four basic conditions).

highly composite number A positive integer having more factors than any smaller positive integer. The first highly composite numbers are 2, 4, 6, 12, 24, and 36; they have 2, 3, 4, 6, 8, and 9 factors, respectively.

Hilbert program Unsuccessful attempt led by David Hilbert to prove that mathematical theory was free from contradiction and to establish a rigorous axiomatic foundation from which all mathematical results could be proven.

Hilbert space An infinite-dimensional vector space whose elements are infinite series that satisfy particular convergence criteria.

incompleteness theorem The principle that every axiomatic mathematical system includes propositions that can neither be proved or disproved.

independent The property of a set of axioms that is satisfied when no one axiom is a logical consequence of the others.

integer A whole number such as -4, -1, 0, 2, or 5.

integral   A function formed as the limit of a sum of terms defined by another function. One of two fundamental ideas of calculus that can be used to find the area under a curve.

integral equation   An equation involving an unknown function and integrals of that function.

integration   The process of determining the integral of a function.

invariant theory   The branch of mathematics concerned with the study of properties that remain fixed when an object is subjected to modifying transformations.

irrational number   A real number such as $\sqrt{2}$ or π that cannot be expressed as a ratio of two integers.

magic square   A square array of numbers for which the sum of the numbers in any row, column, or diagonal is the same.

matrix   A rectangular array of numbers.

mechanics   The branch of physics dealing with the laws of motion.

metric space   A collection of objects for which the distance between any two elements was well defined.

Monte Carlo method   An algorithm that uses random statistical samples to generate approximate numerical solutions.

natural number   One of the positive numbers 1, 2, 3, 4, 5, $\cdots$.

negative number   Any number whose value is less than zero.

noncommutative   The algebraic property of a collection of objects in which two objects combined in one order produce different results from the same two objects combined in the opposite order.

non-Euclidean geometry   A mathematical system of geometry that results from substituting different assumptions in place of the parallel postulate.

number theory   The mathematical study of the properties of positive integers.

numerical analysis   The branch of mathematics concerned with the development and analysis of iterative numerical solutions to mathematical problems.

octal notation   A method using the digits 0, 1, 2, ... , 7 to represent a number as a sum of powers of eight.

odd number   An integer that is not an even number, that cannot be written as two times another integer.

ordinal number   A number indicating the size of a finite or infinite set of objects.

over-perfect number   See ABUNDANT NUMBER.

parallel postulate   The axiom stated by Euclid of Alexandria that for a given point and line, there is only one line that can be drawn through the point that does not eventually meet the given line.

partial differential equation   An equation involving the derivatives of a function of several variables.

partition   A way of expressing a number as a sum of positive integers.

perfect square   See SQUARE NUMBER.

perimeter   The sum of the lengths of the sides of a polygon.

periodic function   A function whose values repeat on a regular basis. A function $f(x)$ is a periodic function if there is some constant k called its period so that $f(x + k) = f(x)$ for all values of x.

pi (π)   The ratio of the circumference a circle to its diameter, approximately 3.14159.

polygon   A planar region bounded by segments. The segments bounding the polygon are its sides, and their endpoints are its vertices.

polyhedron   A solid bounded by polygons. The polygons bounding the polyhedron are its faces; the sides of the polygons are its edges; the vertices of the polygons and its vertices.

polynomial   An algebraic expression that is the sum of the products of numbers and variables.

positive number   Any number whose value is less than zero.

postulate   See AXIOM.

potential theory   The branch of physics dealing with the study of electric, magnetic, and gravitational fields.

power   See EXPONENT.

power series   A representation of a function as an infinite sum of terms in which each term includes a power of the variable.

prime number   An integer greater than one that cannot be divided by any positive integer other than itself and one. The first few prime numbers are 2, 3, 5, 7, 11, 13, 17, $\cdots$.

prime number theorem   The principle of number theory stating that the probability of an integer N being prime is approximately $\dfrac{1}{\ln(N)}$.

probability theory   The branch of mathematics concerned with the systematic determination of numerical values to indicate the likelihood of the occurrence of events.

proof   The logical reasoning that establishes the validity of a theorem from definitions, axioms, and previously proved results.

proper divisor   For any positive integer, those smaller positive numbers that divide it.

pseudoprime   A nonprime positive integer n that divides $2^{n-2} - 2$ without a remainder.

Pythagorean theorem   The rule about right triangles proven by Pythagoras of Samos that states If a, b, and c are the lengths of the three sides of a triangle, then the triangle is a right triangle if and only if $a^2 + b^2 = c^2$.

quantum mechanics   The branch of mathematical physics concerned with the study of subatomic particles.

radius   (1) The distance from the center of a circle to any point on its circumference. (2) A line segment of this length with one endpoint at the center of a circle and the other endpoint located on its circumference.

Ramsey theory   The branch of mathematics concerned with the study of patterns in random collections of data.

ratio   The fraction obtained by dividing one number by another.

rational number   A number that can be expressed as a ratio of two integers. Also known as a fraction.

real number   One of the set of numbers that includes zero, the positive and negative integers, the rationals, and the irrationals.

relativity   The concept in physics concerned with the principles of gravity and motion in accelerated frames of reference.

right angle   An angle with measure 90°.

right triangle   A triangle with one right angle.

root   (1) A solution to an equation. (2) A number that when repeatedly multiplied produces a given numerical value.

round number A number that has many prime factors.

sequence An infinitely long list of values that follow a pattern.

series An infinite sum of numbers or terms.

set A well-defined collection of objects.

set theory The branch of mathematics dealing with relationships between sets.

simultaneous equations Two or more equations relating the same variables that are to be solved at the same time. Also known as a system of equations.

sine For an acute angle in a right triangle, the ratio of the opposite side to the hypotenuse.

special theory of relativity A theory in physics developed by Albert Einstein to explain the properties of space, matter, and time.

sphere The set of all points in three-dimensional space at a given distance, called the radius, from a fixed point, called the center.

square (1) A four-sided polygon with all sides congruent to one another and all angles congruent to one another. (2) To multiply a quantity times itself; raise to the second power.

square number A positive integer that can be written as n^2 for some integer n. Also known as a perfect square.

statistics The branch of mathematics dealing with the collecting, tabulating, and summarizing of numerical information obtained from observational or experimental studies and drawing conclusions about the population from which the data were selected.

stochastic process A statistical technique of estimation that uses randomly selected observations.

subroutine A segment of computer code that instructs the computer to perform specific functions.

surd A numerical expression such as $2 + 5\sqrt{7}$ and $8 - \sqrt[3]{13}$ containing irrational numbers that arise solely from the operations of taking square or higher roots.

symmetry The property of an algebraic expression or a geometrical object for which parts can be interchanged without changing the structure of the expression or object.

system of equations See SIMULTANEOUS EQUATIONS.

tangent For an acute angle in a right triangle, the ratio of the opposite side to the adjacent side.

Tauberian theorem A result about the weighted average of a divergent infinite series.

theorem A mathematical property or rule.

topology The branch of mathematics concerned with the study of the properties of geometrical surfaces.

transcendental number A real number that is not the root of an algebraic equation.

transfinite number A number that gives the cardinality of an infinite set.

triangle A polygon with three vertices and three edges.

triangular number A positive integer that can be written as $1 + 2 + 3 + \cdots + n$ for some integer n.

trigonometric functions The functions $\sin(x)$, $\cos(x)$, and $\tan(x)$ that form the basis of the study of trigonometry.

trigonometry The study of right triangles and the relationships among the measurements of their angles and sides.

Turing machine An abstract machine proposed by Alan Turing as the logical basis for digital computers that moved from one state to another based on the symbols it scanned on a tape, the state it was in, and the rules specified in its operation table.

Turing test An experiment proposed by Alan Turing to determine if a computer possessed artificial intelligence. A person typing at a keyboard sending questions to and receiving responses from a remote source must determine whether the respondent at the other end of the conversation is a human or a computer.

uncountable An infinite set is uncountable if it cannot be put into a one-to-one correspondence with the set of natural numbers.

unit fraction A fraction whose numerator is 1 such as $\frac{1}{2}, \frac{1}{5}$, or $\frac{1}{139}$.

unit interval The set of all real numbers between 0 and 1, written as $[0, 1]$ or as $\left\{x \mid 0 \le x \le 1\right\}$.

unit square The set of all points in the x-y plane whose coordinates lie between 0 and 1, written as $\left\{(x, y) \mid 0 \le x, y \le 1\right\}$.

variable   A letter used to represent an unknown or unspecified quantity.

vertex   The endpoint of a segment in a geometric figure.

volume   The amount of space occupied by a three-dimensional object.

von Neumann algebra   A ring of operators in a Hilbert space.

von Neumann architecture   A design for computers in which the program is electronically stored in the memory of the computer and the hardware is subdivided into five functional units for computation, logical control, memory, input, and output.

FURTHER READING

Books

Ashurst, F. Gareth. *Founders of Modern Mathematics.* London: Muller, 1982. Biographies of selected prominent mathematicians.

Ball, W. W. Rouse. *A Short Account of the History of Mathematics.* New York: Dover, 1960. Reprint of 1908 edition of the classic history of mathematics covering the period from 600 B.C.E. to 1900.

Bell, Eric T. *Men of Mathematics.* New York: Simon and Schuster, 1965. The classic history of European mathematics from 1600 to 1900, organized around the lives of 30 influential mathematicians.

Boyer, Carl, and Uta Merzbach. *A History of Mathematics.* 2d ed. New York: Wiley, 1991. A history of mathematics organized by eras, from prehistoric times through the mid-20th century; for more advanced audiences.

Burton, David M. *The History of Mathematics: An Introduction.* 2d ed. Dubuque, Iowa: Brown, 1988. Very readable college textbook on the history of mathematics through the end of the 19th century, with biographical sketches throughout.

Dunham, William. *Journey Through Genius. The Great Theorems of Mathematics.* New York: Wiley, 1990. Presentation of 12 mathematical ideas focusing on their historical development, the lives of the mathematicians involved, and the proofs of these theorems.

————. *The Mathematical Universe. An Alphabetical Journey through the Great Proofs, Problems, and Personalities.* New York: Wiley, 1994. Presentation of 26 topics in mathematics focusing on their historical development, the lives of the mathematicians involved, and the reasons these theorems are valid.

Eves, Howard. *Great Moments in Mathematics (After 1650).* Washington, D.C.: Mathematical Association of America, 1981. Presentation of major mathematical discoveries that occurred after 1650 and the mathematicians involved.

————. *Great Moments in Mathematics (Before 1650).* Washington, D.C.: Mathematical Association of America, 1983. Presentation of 20 major mathematical discoveries that occurred before 1650 and the mathematicians involved.

————. *An Introduction to the History of Mathematics.* 3d ed. New York: Holt, Rinehart and Winston, 1969. An undergraduate textbook covering the history of mathematical topics through elementary calculus, accessible to high school students.

Gillispie, Charles C., ed. *Dictionary of Scientific Biography.* 18 vols. New York: Scribner, 1970–80. Multivolume encyclopedia presenting biographies of thousands of mathematicians and scientists, for adult audiences.

Grinstein, Louise S., and Paul J. Campbell, eds. *Women of Mathematics: A Biobibliographic Sourcebook.* New York: Greenwood Press, 1987. Biographical profiles of 43 women, each with an extensive list of references.

Henderson, Harry. *Modern Mathematicians.* New York: Facts On File, 1996. Profiles of 13 mathematicians from the 19th and 20th centuries.

James, Ioan M. *Remarkable Mathematicians: From Euler to von Neumann.* Cambridge: Cambridge University Press, 2002. Profiles of 60 mathematicians from the 18th, 19th, and 20th centuries.

Katz, Victor J. *A History of Mathematics: An Introduction.* 2d ed. Reading, Mass.: Addison-Wesley Longman, 1998. College textbook that explains accessible portions of mathematical works and provides brief biographical sketches.

Morrow, Charlene, and Teri Perl, eds. *Notable Women in Mathematics: A Biographical Dictionary*. Westport, Conn.: Greenwood Press, 1998. Short biographies of 59 women mathematicians including many 20th-century figures.

Muir, Jane. *Of Men and Numbers: The Story of the Great Mathematicians*. New York: Dover, 1996. Short profiles of mathematicians.

Newman, James R., ed. *The World of Mathematics*. 4 vols. New York: Simon and Schuster, 1956. Collection of essays about topics in mathematics, including the history of mathematics.

Osen, Lynn M. *Women in Mathematics*. Cambridge, Mass.: MIT Press, 1974. Biographies of eight women mathematicians through the early 20th century.

Perl, Teri. *Math Equals: Biographies of Women Mathematicians + Related Activities*. Menlo Park, Calif.: Addison-Wesley, 1978. Biographies of 10 women mathematicians, through the early 20th century, each accompanied by exercises related to their mathematical work.

Reimer, Luetta, and Wilbert Reimer. *Historical Connections in Mathematics*. 2 vols. Fresno, Calif.: AIMS Educational Foundation, 1992–93. Each volume includes brief portraits of 10 mathematicians with worksheets related to their mathematical discoveries; for elementary school students.

———. *Mathematicians Are People, Too: Stories from the Lives of Great Mathematicians*. Parsippany, N.J.: Seymour, 1990. Collection of stories about 15 mathematicians with historical facts and fictionalized dialogue; intended for elementary school students.

———. *Mathematicians Are People, Too: Stories from the Lives of Great Mathematicians*. Vol. 2. Parsippany, N.J.: Seymour, 1995. Collection of stories about another 15 mathematicians, with historical facts and fictionalized dialogue, intended for elementary school students.

Segal, Sanford L. *Mathematicians under the Nazis*. Princeton, N.J.: Princeton University Press, 2003. Details the dismantling of the mathematical community of scholars in Germany under Adolf Hitler's leadership.

Stillwell, John. *Mathematics and Its History*. New York: Springer-Verlag, 1989. Undergraduate textbook organized around 20 topics, each developed in their historical context.

Struik, Dirk J. *A Source Book in Mathematics, 1200–1800*. Cambridge, Mass.: Harvard University Press, 1969. Excerpts with commentary from 75 of the influential mathematical manuscripts of the period.

———. *A Concise History of Mathematics*. 4th rev. ed. New York: Dover, 1987. Brief history of mathematics through the first half of the 20th century with extensive multilingual biographical references.

Tabak, John. *The History of Mathematics*. 5 vols. New York: Facts On File, 2004. Important events and prominent individuals in the development of the major branches of mathematics; for grades 6 and up.

Tanton, James. *Encyclopedia of Mathematics*. New York: Facts On File, 2005. Articles and essays about events, ideas, and people in mathematics; for grades 9 and up.

Turnbull, Herbert W. *The Great Mathematicians*. New York: New York University Press, 1961. Profiles of six mathematicians with more detail than most sources.

Young, Robyn V., ed. *Notable Mathematicians: From Ancient Times to the Present*. Detroit, Mich.: Gale, 1998. Short profiles of mathematicians.

Internet Resources

Agnes Scott College. "Biographies of Women Mathematicians." Available online. URL: http://www.agnesscott.edu/lriddle/women/women.htm. Accessed March 4, 2005. Biographies of more than 100 women mathematicians prepared by students at Agnes Scott College, Decatur, Georgia.

Bellevue Community College. "Mathographies." Available online. URL: http://scidiv.bcc.ctc.edu/Math/MathFolks.html. Accessed March 4, 2005. Brief biographies of 25 mathematicians prepared by faculty members at Bellevue Community College, Washington.

Drexel University. "Math Forum." Available online. URL: http://www.mathforum.org. Accessed March 3, 2005. Site for mathematics and mathematics education that includes "Problem of the Week," "Ask Dr. Math," and the Historia-Matematica discussion group, by the School of Education at Drexel University, Philadelphia.

Miller, Jeff. "Images of Mathematicians on Postage Stamps." Available online. URL: http://jeff560.tripod.com. Accessed March 6, 2005. Images of hundreds of mathematicians and mathematical topics on international stamps with link to an online ring of mathematical stamp collectors, by high school math teacher Jeff Miller.

National Association of Mathematics. "Mathematicians of the African Diaspora." Available online. URL: http://www.math.buffalo.edu/mad. Accessed March 1, 2005. Includes profiles of 250 black mathematicians and historical information about mathematics in ancient Africa.

Rice University. "Galileo Project Catalog of the Scientific Community in the 16th and 17th Centuries." Available online. URL: http://galileo.rice.edu/lib/catalog.html. Accessed July 5, 2005. Biographical outlines of 600 mathematicians and scientists of the period, compiled by the late professor Richard Westfall of Indiana University.

Scienceworld. "Eric Weisstein's World of Scientific Biography." Available online. URL: http://scienceworld.wolfram.com/biography. Accessed February 12, 2005. Brief profiles of more than 250 mathematicians and hundreds of other scientists. Link to related site Mathworld, an interactive mathematics encyclopedia providing access to numerous articles about historical topics and extensive discussions of mathematical terms and ideas, by Eric Weisstein of Wolfram Research.

Simon Fraser University. "History of Mathematics." Available online. URL: http://www.math.sfu.ca/histmath. Accessed January 19, 2005. A collection of short profiles of a dozen mathematicians, from Simon Fraser University, Burnaby, British Columbia, Canada.

University of Saint Andrews. "MacTutor History of Mathematics Archive." Available online. URL: http://www-groups.dcs.st-andrews.ac.uk/~history. Accessed March 5, 2005. Searchable online index of mathematical history and biographies of more than 2,000 mathematicians, from the University of Saint Andrews, in Scotland.

University of Tennessee. "Math Archives." Available online. URL: http://archives.math.utk.edu/topics/history.html. Accessed December 10, 2004. Ideas for teaching mathematics and links to Web sites about the history of mathematics and other mathematical topics, by the University of Tennessee, Knoxville.

Wikipedia: The Free Encyclopedia. "Mathematics." Available online. URL: http://en.wikipedia.org/wiki/Mathematics. Accessed August 22, 2005. Includes biographies with many links to in-depth explanations of related mathematical topics.

ASSOCIATIONS

Association for Women in Mathematics, 4114 Computer and Space Sciences Building, University of Maryland, College Park, MD 20742-2461. Web site: http://www.awm-math.org. Telephone: (301) 405-7892. Professional society for female mathematics professors. Web site includes link to biographies of women in mathematics.

Mathematical Association of America, 1529 18th Street NW, Washington, DC 20036. Web site: http://www.maa.org. Telephone: (202) 387-5200. Professional society for college mathematics professors. Web site includes link to the association's History of Mathematics Special Interest Group (HOM SIGMAA).

National Association of Mathematicians, Department of Mathematics, 244 Mathematics Building, University at Buffalo, Buffalo, NY 14260-2900. Web site: http://www.math.buffalo.edu/mad/NAM. Professional society focusing on needs of under-represented American minorities in mathematics.

National Council of Teachers of Mathematics, 1906 Association Drive, Reston, VA 20191-1502. Web site: http://www.nctm.org. Telephone: (703) 620-9840. Professional society for mathematics teachers.

Index